Praise for *Crossroads of Conjure*

"We often talk about magic in the context of our workings. While we can often name magics from foreign lands, like Celtic, Nordic, Roman, etc., it is easy to forget that all magic, at some point, is local. In *Crossroads of Conjure*, Katrina Rasbold expertly describes some folk magics that are much closer to our North American home. The thoroughness of this book opens new vistas for the reader—I know it did for me."

—Rev. Jean (Drum) Pagano, Archdruid ADF

"Katrina Rasbold takes us on a road trip of pure Americana magic. … *Crossroads of Conjure* reveals the often overlooked and misunderstood, yet deeply powerful folk magic born and bred in the good ol' USA, proving that witchcraft and spell-work really are as American as apple pie."

—Tomás Prower, author of *La Santa Muerte*

"*Crossroads of Conjure* by Katrina Rasbold is like a walking tour through the times and places of distinct but related systems of spiritual power led by a seasoned traveler. Let Katrina be your guide and you'll find what you want."

—Ivo Dominguez Jr, author of *Keys to Perception*

"Katrina Rasbold has written a brave, beautiful, balanced book.... [She] brings a winning combination of in-depth historical research, cultural sensitivity, and personal experience.... Her knowledge of her subjects is equaled by her passion. Every page is suffused with fierce love. Whether you are called to study Conjure yourself or simply wish to gain a deeper understanding of these ancient and evolving arts, this book is for you."

—Elizabeth Cunningham, author of *The Maeve Chronicles*

CROSSROADS
── of ──
CONJURE

© Myk Aero

About the Author

Katrina Rasbold is the author of over thirty books, including eighteen on various aspects of the magical arts. She also pens the popular fictional series The Seven Sisters of Avalon, as well as other fictional and nonfictional works.

Born in the hills of Kentucky and raised around folk magic, Katrina studied the magical arts all over the world, including in the Marianas Islands and the UK, before settling in her current home in the forested Eden of the High Sierra Mountains of California. She has taught classes throughout the world and frequently teaches at PantheaCon in San Jose, as well as at Sacramento Pagan Pride and PanGaia Festival in Fair Oaks, California. She currently teaches classes with her husband,

Eric Rasbold, at LightWeavers Academy in Citrus Heights, California.

She and Eric are co-creators of the CUSP spiritual path, a detailed magical structure using the ancient agricultural holidays to create positive life change year after year. They co-authored the Bio-Universal Energy Series and their first book, *Energy Magic*, spent several weeks on the Amazon Best Seller list for Neopaganism upon its release in 2013. They are founding members of the non-profit organization North Western Circles Association, which raises money to benefit the Sacramento Wildlife Center.

In addition to writing and lecturing, Katrina works as a professional bruja and conjure woman, and for years, she and Eric owned the shop Two Sisters Botánica in Roseville, California. She now has an online store where they sell handmade magical products and offer their services. (Find it at twosistersbotanica.com) They have six adult children who are grown up and loose out there in the world.

CROSSROADS
—— of ——
CONJURE

The Roots and Practices of Granny Magic, Hoodoo, Brujería, and Curanderismo

KATRINA RASBOLD

Llewellyn Worldwide
Woodbury, Minnesota

First Edition
Second Printing, 2019

Cover design by Shira Atakpu
Editing by Annie Burdick

Llewellyn Publications is a registered trademark of Llewellyn Worldwide Ltd.

Library of Congress Cataloging-in-Publication Data
Names: Rasbold, Katrina, author.
Title: Crossroads of conjure : the roots and practices of Granny Magic, Hoodoo, Brujer?ia, and Curanderismo / by Katrina Rasbold.
Description: First edition. | Woodbury, Minnesota : Llewellyn Worldwide, [2019] | Includes bibliographical references and index.
Identifiers: LCCN 2018044212 (print) | LCCN 2018049898 (ebook) | ISBN 9780738758244 (ebook) | ISBN 9780738757865 (alk. paper)
Subjects: LCSH: Magic--United States. | Healers--United States. | Folk religion--United States.
Classification: LCC BF1434.U6 (ebook) | LCC BF1434.U6 R37 2019 (print) | DDC 133.4/30973—dc23
LC record available at https://lccn.loc.gov/2018044212

Llewellyn Publications
A Division of Llewellyn Worldwide Ltd.
2143 Woodale Drive
Woodbury, MN 55125-2989
www.llewellyn.com

Printed in the United States of America

This book is dedicated to my maternal grandmother, Mary Frances "Granny" Mitchell, with great thanks for all she taught me and a love and respect that spans the generations and veils that separate us. What I wouldn't give to have her hug me around the neck just one more time.

Acknowledgments

My deepest gratitude goes out to Don Francisco, Don Fuji, Doña Marta, and Doña Queta, whose influences made me the practitioner that I am today.

Additionally, I would like to thank my Hoodoo mentors, Hexeba Theaux and Maya Gray, for their dedication to the craft of Conjure that called us and for the kindness they showed in sharing their wisdom and experience with me.

Above all, this book is dedicated to my husband, Eric Rasbold, who never lost faith in me as a writer and whose tireless translations of Spanish language texts on Brujería and Curanderismo made this book a far better package.

CONTENTS

DISCLAIMER

The information contained in this book derives from historical folk belief and practice. It is not intended to take the place of qualified medical care and no guarantees are implied or extended. The author and publisher are not liable for any injury or other malady resulting from the application of the information contained within this book. Please use common sense if and when attempting these practices and consult a healthcare professional when needed. The folk magic practices discussed in this book may seem simple, but they are normally conveyed through an apprentice relationship with a qualified teacher. If you feel a sincere calling to any of these practices, it is important that you do not attempt the techniques without training. If you are ready, a teacher will come to you. Put your beacon out into the world and trust the process.

INTRODUCTION

When we think of magical practice, European and Middle Eastern traditions are often what come to mind. The many branches of Wicca, as well as Druidism, Ásatrú, and other Neopagan practices have great publicists and now constitute the status quo in conversations about nature-based spirituality.

It is equally tempting to imagine that all magical practices are either Pagan- or Heathen-based, or that they are all reconstructed versions of lost medieval religions. What we may fail to consider is that some of the strongest and most vibrant folk magic cultures, including Hoodoo, Granny Magic, Curanderismo, and Brujería, all covered in this book, are not Pagan at all, and despite having roots in other parts of the world, primarily developed in the United States.

Brujería and Curanderismo across the American Southwest, Hoodoo in the Gulf area and Southeast, and Appalachian Granny Magic throughout the Eastern United States all form a strong, interwoven network of folk magic practices rooted in a syncretized Christian foundation. These practices flourished during a time when they were needed most, enduring to our modern age due to the layering of historic conjuring and healing techniques onto the foundation of the more socially acceptable Christian precepts.

Although Hoodoo is the system one usually refers to when speaking of "Conjure" as a practice, the New Orleans branch of Hoodoo and Voodoo practice, the Cajun traiteur healers, Appalachian and Ozark folk magic, Native American practices, and the Gullah Geechee of South Carolina are all also technically forms of Conjure. Conjure is a broad term much like "Paganism" or "Christianity" in its application, encompassing a large scope of traditions and modalities with unifying commonalities.

Each of these folk magic systems has its own unique presentation; and yet, the Conjure cultures explored in this book share many interconnecting aspects, the most dominant being that they developed in adversity and were created by disadvantaged people. These magical pioneers did not establish these practices with an aim of creating a vital magical system that would endure through the ages. Their ambitions were quite immediate and basic: to stay alive, preserve their remaining dignity, and foster what quality of life they could build within those challenging circumstances. The magical perspectives presented here were nothing less than survival tools built on the premise of healing and effective management of the day-to-day issues of life. They address marriage, child-rearing, employment, safety, protection, health, and crisis intervention.

Few, if any, of the practitioners of these traditions were affluent or privileged people. Most lived in poverty and used their Conjure skills to create a tolerable life within largely untenable circumstances. To understand and embrace the nature and development of these paths, we must confront and identify with the life experiences of those who laid the foundations that allowed the paths not only to unfold but to endure. To varying degrees, these paths are still practiced today, which is a testimony not only to the solid foundations on which they were built, but also to their adaptability in the face of sometimes extreme societal and cultural changes.

In our modern magical society, we use phrases such as "spiritual path" or "magical practice" to identify the religious or practical application of our spellwork and celebratory events. The people who created the processes and modalities discussed in this book would not and did not use terms such as these. What we consider "spellwork" or "magical practice" was simply "life" for them. They saw no delineation between the secular and the spiritual life and did not create separate terminology to isolate their use of charms or other workings. It was simply "what was." The identification of any practices described in this book as "magical" or "spellwork" is *my* usage of the words that *we* now use, rather than how the developing or even current cultures represented here would label their experiences, beliefs, or techniques.

As we explore Granny Magic, Hoodoo, Curanderismo, and Brujería—the primary presentations of folk magic in the American South—we see common threads that bind them together:

- Survival through adaptation and the syncretization of cultural and regional folk traditions onto the more socially acceptable Christian faith

- Vehement rejection of any affiliation with Paganism, Witchcraft, or Heathenism in favor of full Christian identification

- Advocacy for magical defense, even to the extreme of justifying death curses or other calamities against those who work against them or seek to harm hearth, home, or security

- Beginnings born of extreme adversity to address the very basic needs for survival, with a strong emphasis on medical and healthcare practices

- Basic, locally accessible components for spellwork, usually derived from natural sources easily available to the practitioner

- Magical work that emphasizes mundane life issues rather than spiritual development or any type of self-actualization

- No concept of karma, three-fold law, or other forms of divine retribution within the theology

- Matrilineal perspective without any gender exclusivity to practices, although certain roles more commonly fall to specific genders

- Information and instruction conveyed through oral and practical means rather than written

Folk magic was rarely a mere celebration of the turning of the seasons or a hopeful wish for a better life. These people did not cast circles, call quarters, or recreate the cosmos in their sacred space. American folk magic in the 1700s–1800s and even into the early 1900s addressed matters of life and death, of survival and protection, and of healing and warding. As we explore these practices, we can scarcely imagine how different our own lives are from those who developed these folk magic techniques amid extreme poverty and oppression.

Not quite as far back as the 1700–1800s are my own memories of growing up in rural Kentucky in the 1960s, surrounded by homegrown wisdom, storytelling, cyclical harvest celebrations, and abject poverty.

My childhood was devoid of any thoughts or mention of magic, Paganism, or other forms of mysticism. Our neighbors and my family spoke of ghosts and haints, of ways to heal without using "store-bought" pharmaceuticals, and of the power of prayer and charms. Most of their cures for injury or ailments started with something like, "First, go find some horse dung…" or "You will need some horehound candy for that cough or it is going to stay for weeks." Their colloquial wisdom sounded something like, "You can take the town doctor's medicine for that summer cold and it will be gone in a week or you can use home medicine and it will be gone in seven days."

Until I was an adult and living on the other side of the world, the only hint I ever saw that witches might exist, beyond a scare tactic for unruly children or as fairy tale villains, was when I found a book about "real" Witches between my mother's mattress and box spring. I was fascinated by the narrow set of glossy pages in the middle of the book that depicted their rituals in black and white photos. I was sure that magic like the book described was fictional and the images in the book must be posed. Besides, magic was not *real*...and yet, "magic," as I would later come to know it, was all around me. I just did not yet have a label for it.

I treasure the memories I have of growing up in rural Kentucky, locked into poverty with only the tools of scripture, charms, hard work, and faith to help make life better. The people I knew never aspired to be or have more than they did and looked down on those who did so. Their position in society came not from what they had, but from who they were and how they behaved in the world. Anyone who tried to achieve wealth or outdistance their own social class received the odious distinction of "gettin' above their raisin'."

The lineage leading to my birth in Augusta, Kentucky, in 1961 was of Scotch-Irish and Native American extraction, as well as some high-born, snooty English thrown in the mix, although they were long bred out by the time I came along.

No one in our line had been well-to-do for generations. We were about as dirt poor as you could get, but my own family was sufficiently affluent for me to be able to get a new pair of shoes when I started school each year and a large navel orange in the toe of my Christmas stocking *without fail*. My mother made all of our clothes, and I did not own a pair of blue jeans until the ninth grade when my father found a pair that fit me in the dumpster where the Salvation Army discarded the clothes they could not sell in their thrift shop due to disrepair. Mom covered the holes in the jeans with cloth images she cut from tea towels and I could not possibly have been prouder.

We heated our homes with the bituminous coal that my grandfather mined out of the earth himself and sold by the bucketful to neighbors. I did not then consider the energy in the flowers, the weeds, and the roots of the land we used to heal. Our "magic" came from prayer, the power of words, and the "laying on of hands," and we depended on it every single day. And yet, to us, it was not magic. It was the healing power God gave to us through his mercy, embedded into nature.

Reciting scripture and prayer truly could heal pretty much any injury or illness, and superstition was not a joke at all, nor did it even elicit as much as a nervous laugh. It was a promise. If you sang at the table or whistled in the bed, the Devil would most assuredly take you *before* you were dead. We feared nothing as much as we feared Satan and the loss of our everlasting souls. We never let anyone except the Tooth Fairy take our baby teeth because something very bad would happen. What exact form that overwhelming "bad" would take was unclear, but *very bad* it would certainly be.

Peeling an apple fully in one careful spiral without once having the peeling break meant we would marry well. We stored brooms with bristles up or horizontally across the fireplace to keep the bad things from flying into the house through the chimney. The only thing I ever saw come through the chimney was an unfortunately misdirected sparrow, but that meant the broom worked, so we called it a win.

Onion poultices healed infections, and horse manure inside of an ace bandage would fix a sprained ankle right up. We always kept the cats out of a baby's crib so they could not steal the child's breath as it slept, and we would never dream of whistling as we walked past a graveyard or entering one after dusk, lest we offend the spirits. Not to mention that if a woman whistled, she might just call up a powerful wind.

We had "singings" and barn dances, and in the fall we risked life and limb riding on hay bales stacked onto flatbed trailers and pulled by tractors around the town in a tradition called a hayride. New couples formed each hayride season as sweethearts found their way to one another in the fragrant, stiff straw.

In my teenage years, my interest was in the paranormal, in haints and ghosts and specters and shades. My paternal grandmother, Grandma Chapman, who went to seminary school and was a terrifying ordained Pilgrim Holiness minister, cultivated this interest by filling my library with every book she could locate on the subject. She gave me a doll she pulled from the Ohio River after a flood, which she claimed was haunted, although I never detected any supernatural activity around her. I named the doll Esther, after my grandmother's middle name, and I think she might haunt me now because I have seen versions of her easily seven or eight times in various thrift stores across the country (the doll, not my grandmother).

While living in England, I was fortunate to have the singularly unique experience of learning from traditional British Witches (as opposed to British Traditional Witches) and then, upon my return to the United States, I immersed myself into Wicca for many years. I hosted my own circles for close to thirty years, the past twenty while practicing CUSP (Climbing Up the Spiral Pathway), a spiritual path based primarily on what I learned in England and elsewhere along the way, merged with what my husband gleaned as an avid student of how humans interact with the Divine.

Years ago, in tandem with my work in CUSP, I began the study of Rootwork/Hoodoo, first on my own and then under the tutelage of two experienced Hoodoo mentors. Later, through a series of serendipitous and sacred events, I received my calling as a bruja and began my practice as a bruja in my shop in Roseville, California, and then later away from storefront practice and into an online teaching and working interface. I am honored to have received the title of "curandera," a title in the Latino culture identifying a spiritual healer, from those people I helped over the years.

Blending my Granny Magic origins (the first exposure I ever had to magic without even realizing it was magic) with my Hoodoo and Brujería vocation fulfills me in a way I never imagined. Several years ago, the idea struck me that if an old Witch like myself could feel such joy from these practices born right here in the United States, perhaps others could as well. What started as a workshop presentation on folk magic in the American South eventually became this book, which I present to you with fierce love and devotion.

Although throughout this text I share with the reader some of my own experiences of living a magical life as a practitioner of these traditions, the focus of this work is not on how to become a bruja, a curandero, a rootworker, or a granny doctor. Those who feel called to any of these vibrant and effective applications of natural energy should seek out a competent and experienced practitioner of that specific art to act as a mentor.

An apprentice of Brujería, Curanderismo, Appalachian Granny Magic, or Hoodoo learns far more than what can be found in a simple spellbook. The practice is as much about the focused and spiritual application of energy and will as it is about which herbs and oils go into the formula of a floor wash. Under a skilled hand, the apprentice learns to fully immerse him or herself into the practices and to embody the path with honor, especially if it is not connected to his or her own ancestry. These gifts come from someone who has mastered the individual crafts and has themselves walked the path with dignity and integrity.

This book is an exploration of how these American folk magic entities formed and the ways the people who created them used the techniques for protection, healing, and survival. It is a celebration of the sustainability of these systems of Conjure and the dispelling of myths and misunderstandings that surround them. As our understanding grows of how these practices not only developed, but survived, we can also see why there is currently a resurgence of interest in their use in today's uncertain times. Created in conditions of disadvantage, it makes sense that our focus would return to those time-proven Conjure techniques as economic disadvantage affects even more people in our changing world.

The narrative involving the historical development of these traditions is complicated, to say the least. I do not presume to present my findings as the only truths, and others may have conflicting information. The information you read here comes from years of concerted research, and what I offer are some of the truths that find mostly unified consensus among those who honor and carry forward the individual paths into their current presentations.

Ethics in Folk Magic Practice

As the current worldwide economic turndown creates personal hardship for a greater number of people, many of whom are accustomed to affluence, it is no accident that we see a return to the more "grassroots" forms of magical practice that originated out of adversity. Conditioned as we are toward conventional magical ethics, the lack of imposed ethical restrictions in these magical practices may seem harsh and even primitive. When considered at the most basic level, however, one can see that the lack of indoctrinated ethical boundaries results in an outcome of greater, rather than less, personal discipline.

Stage magician and performer Penn Jillette is a vocal and dedicated atheist who speaks openly and eloquently about his lack of religious attachment to morality. He says people often ask him, if he has no god or no higher power governing him, what keeps him from raping and killing all he wants to? His response is that he *does* rape and kill as much as he wants to, which is to say not at all, because he is neither a rapist nor a killer.

The misperception is that if people do not have an overlying religious dictate to keep them from doing horrible things, they will run willy-nilly into the debauchery of evil, simply because they can do so without fear of divine retribution. On the contrary, the very knowledge of their magical power and what they can do with it gives the people I have known who walk these unregulated paths an even greater sense of caution and a deeper consideration of their magical actions.

This ideology was a significant step for me to process when I transitioned from Wiccan practice into Rootwork and Brujería. Just as moving from Christianity to Wicca was challenging in some ways, so was the ethical shift from Wicca into folk magic practice. It was jarring, but once I processed the implications and considerations, it felt organic and right to me. It will not feel so to everyone, and that is the beauty of working in and with a community of varied practices. There is room for everyone.

When exploring magical ethics, one must consider the concept of reasonable defense. If someone came into my home to hurt me or the people I care about and I had the power to stop it, but chose not to do so, then I would also be culpable in the attack. Likewise, if someone was harming me or another person and I could do something about it magically, I would take that step without consideration of a "harm none" or three-fold law policy.

The gray area is that what constitutes malicious harm versus reasonable defense is quite subjective, and the difference between culpability and innocent bystanding is often a matter of opinion. It is up to the practitioner to decide if a work is appropriate to the circumstances and whether it fits into their own ethical construct. As a forewarning, however, none of the folk magic systems we discuss in this book are fond of turning the other cheek or blessing their antagonists with love and light and sending them on their way.

As we delve into the history and practice of Appalachian Granny Magic, Hoodoo, Curanderismo, and Brujería, some of the modalities and mindsets may feel uncomfortable to those who are used to a more ethically dogmatic theology. Take a breath, open your mind, and imagine the perspective of the practitioner. Sometimes in considering the philosophies of other paths we galvanize our own beliefs or, perhaps, expand them as we integrate new ideas.

I often quote author and professional blogger John Beckett, who says, "Don't be afraid to get your hands dirty, but don't forget to wash your hands." Folk magic involves the essentials of taking care of business. To the minds of those who work in Conjure fields, sometimes taking care of business involves wielding energy in a punitive fashion.

Just as the energy that runs through the electrical circuits in your home is neutral, magical energy is also benign until it filters through the intentions of the practitioner who wields it. Electricity can warm your home or it can electrocute a person. In either instance, it is not the energy itself that is baneful or benevolent. It is merely energy. A gun or a knife is not evil, but people can do evil things with those tools. Likewise, they can defend their loved ones with the same knife or gun. A knife or gun used carelessly can inadvertently harm in ways unintended. Magic is the same, and with the use of divine power comes personal responsibility.

Each person has their own code of ethics and beliefs about what is right and what is wrong. "Left-handed magic," "dark magic," or other words used to describe any magic act that others find objectionable are equally subjective concepts. This degree of interpretive analysis is why, even within magical paths that *do* follow documented edicts regarding ethics, it can still be difficult to establish a clear consensus.

Isaac Bonewits, Pagan pioneer and father of Ár nDraíocht Féin, identifies the term "black magic" as: "A racist, sexist, creedist and classist term used to refer to magic being done for 'evil' purposes or by people of whom the user of the term disapproves" (Bonewits, 249).

His inclusion of the term *racist* in his definition stems from the ongoing identification of Hoodoo as "black magic," which some claim is an orchestrated disparagement of the magical practices of enslaved African Americans to differentiate their works from the "white magic" of Caucasian practitioners. While there remains some debate as to the authenticity of this claim, there is certainly sufficient evidence to support the validity of the assertion.

Gerald Gardner, the father of Wicca, once said, "Magic is in itself neither black nor white, bad nor good; it is how it is used, the intent or the knowledge behind it, that matters" (Gardner 2004, 15).

Documentary filmmaker Alex Mar quotes Victor Anderson, the creator of the Feri Tradition, as saying, "Poetry is white magic. Black magic is anything that works." In the same text, Mar cites the consummate bard, Gwydion Pendderwen's statement that "He who cannot blast cannot bless" (Mar 2016, 217).

Like those quoted above, many of the pioneers of modern Paganism advocate for a full-spectrum practice and ascribe to the notion that one must know how to walk in the shadows to appreciate the light.

Is there baneful magic? Absolutely. Are there those within these folk magic practices whose morality is in question by rational people or even the most generous-minded of magical practitioners? Most certainly. In all cultures and all religions, there are people who abuse power, spiritual and otherwise, to meddle in the lives of others. Folk magic communities are no different.

During my early years as a Christian, I listened with horror to some of the passionate and sincere prayers offered up by those in our congregation attempting to control the lives of others. The answers to whether magic is "good" or "bad" are as varied as whether *people* are "good" or "bad," and to my own observation, there seems to be little relevance to the spiritual or magical path a person follows when evaluating their "goodness" or their "badness."

In Hoodoo practice, we consider a work to be "justified" or "not justified." This seems a safe path to follow, since it identifies a reaction subjective to a specific set of circumstances. Is it justified to bind a person who threatens to go after your job? Is it justified to reflect and return baneful energy sent to you? Is it justified to break up the affair between your wife and another man?

Different people will give you different answers, and while one magical practitioner would say there is never a reason to interfere with the free will of others, another will tell you that magical defense is the responsibility of every practitioner. These two opinions, which seem in opposition to one another, could easily come from members of the same magical path or even the same magical working group.

This sort of incongruent thought is why the distinction of "black magic" and "white magic" does not hold up under careful analytical scrutiny. Casting aside the potentially distasteful and racist implications of the terms, there is no direct dogma or pseudo-catechism defining the gray areas within the moral concepts of magic. Each practitioner must determine this within their own spirit.

In keeping with that idea, this book rejects the concepts of "white magic" versus "black magic" or any ethical condemnation and instead focuses on the specific circumstances that cause a person to take extreme magical action either in defense or aggression.

PART 1

HOODOO

──── 1 ────
About Hoodoo

M ore than any of the other three folk magic systems we explore in this book, Hoodoo is a living, breathing tradition that experienced an ongoing process of evolution and synthesis as societal and cultural influences brought incredible pressure to bear. Throughout its stages of development, those within the practice faced untenable oppression. And yet Hoodoo endured.

As we explore the development of Hoodoo, or "Rootworking" as it is also known, we chart a course through treacherous waters. Whereas Appalachian Granny Magic, Brujería, and Curanderismo have a relatively known and undisputed history, in Hoodoo there are what I can only describe as "multiple truths." Although my intention is to find the middle road that is mostly accurate, I in no way hold up what I present as the only truth, and it's certainly not everyone's truth. It is almost impossible to make definitive statements about the history and development of Hoodoo without offending the understood facts of another historian or rootworker. I will, however, do my best to present a reasonable composite view of the history and development of this heavily nuanced folk magic system.

The most commonly agreed upon description of Hoodoo is that it is an amalgamated folk magic practice developed in the United States on a foundation of the traditional healing and spiritual modalities of Central and West Africa, with varying degrees of European and Caribbean influences and integrations. The degree and value of the non-African components, as well as the involvement of non-Christian rootworkers in a previously fully Christianized healing and spiritual process, fuel intense arguments among Hoodoo practitioners.

A recent revival of interest in Hoodoo attracted many students who have no ancestral connection to any aspect of the practice, much to the ire and derision of some who do. Divisive issues such as these create a hotbed of conflict within the Hoodoo community. Most rootworkers, however, find their own stride and thrive within this powerful and vibrant practice. In its modern presentation, Hoodoo represents a large and varied network of magical techniques and traditions.

Hoodoo is a perfect example of history being written by the victors. A good bit of what we know about Hoodoo comes from whitewashed—and that pun is quite intentional—versions of the story of this folk magic system, often with the underlying motive of legitimizing the involvement of and contributions by non-African American rootworkers.

I speak as a Caucasian rootworker who received a calling and followed it into active practice despite my concerns about accusations of appropriation. I honor those who question my place within the Hoodoo community and understand why they feel that way. I feel strongly about presenting the development of Hoodoo from the most reliable sources available, and it is from that perspective that I write this book.

For over three hundred years, the transatlantic slave trade forcefully relocated indigenous people from the Western coast of Africa to the eastern, southeastern, and Gulf areas of the United States, as well as to Haiti, Cuba, the West Indies, and Latin America. It is estimated that over 12.5 million Africans were kidnapped and transported by ship to these areas, with over two million of them dying en route, due to the horrific conditions onboard. Although this information is familiar to most readers of this book, I restate it because it is vital that at a minimum, an academic awareness of the conditions that created what we now know as Hoodoo remains in the forefront of our minds as we explore its history.

Each individual African region had its own set of spiritual and healing practices, with similarities to and differences from those in surrounding areas. Through inaccurate societal and media representations, many people think of the captured slaves as uncivilized people who were little more than animals. In my own childhood in the early 1960s in rural Kentucky, there were people who lived around me who truly believed that African American people had tails. This sort of thinking comes as the result of an aggressive campaign of untruths spread by those who traded, sold, and kept slaves, to justify the poor treatment of their chattel. If they depicted the people they sold as more animal than human, there was no reason to afford them the dignity and rights of a human being.

Hollywood especially portrays the African slave as ignorant, superstitious, and even feral, when in fact, many of the captured Africans brought into the American South came from organized, hierarchical, and structured cultures. Within these cultures, charms, chants, and other practices we would now call magical governed medical treatments, including successful surgeries. These magical practices also dictated social experiences such as relationship management among families and neighbors, the mediation of disputes, hunting, animal husbandry, and the cycles of life (including the management of birth, pubescence, marriage arrangements, and formal burials). Among those captured were healers, surgeons, midwives, blacksmiths, hunters, trackers, shamans, cooks, priests, and musicians, many of whom had honored positions in their homelands.

If you ask a contemporary rootworker to define Hoodoo, their interpretation often includes a strong distinction of Hoodoo from any religious connotations, isolating Hoodoo as a magical practice devoid of ties to any religion or spirituality. While that might be the case in today's presentation of Hoodoo, it was not always so. This position over-simplifies the roots of Hoodoo, which was, in its early development, a deeply spiritual process. In the African cultures from which

Hoodoo derived, the spiritual life merged so deeply into the mundane that the secular and the sacred were nearly inseparable.

Slave traders delivered their human cargo to different ports of call throughout the Americas, and the African diaspora began. Traumatized and often near death from the neglect and mistreatment aboard slave ships, these Africans settled onto plantations or other work arenas, bringing nothing but their memories of the homeland and their knowledge of healing and conjuring.

Almost immediately, cultural diffusion began, as retained memories and shared information spread among the displaced Africans, with geographical and cultural variances blending into common and accepted practices. Forced to adapt their healing processes to the vastly different flora, fauna, and roots in America, the now mixed African cultures commingled their sacred chants, recipes, charms, dances, healing modalities, and common societal theologies such as the veneration of nature, elders, and the ancestral dead. With no hope of replicating what they left behind, they developed something new, which would eventually come to be known as Hoodoo.

In some locations, slave owners had friendly relations with Native American tribes, many of which owned slaves, were slaves, married slaves, and/or hid slaves. The familiarity of Native Americans with the healing herbs and roots indigenous to the area helped the displaced African healers learn appropriate substitutions for the natural pharmacopeia used in Africa.

Author, diligent researcher, and professor at Rutgers State University, Katrina Hazzard-Donald writes, "[Hoodoo] was a glue that held the slave community together" (Hazzard-Donald 2013, 15). Hoodoo served not only as a system of medical, psychological, and spiritual treatment, but defined the uniqueness of a culture facing aggressive and abusive pressure to mainstream into a society that offered them no respite or acceptance.

Hazzard-Donald defines Hoodoo as "the indigenous, herbal, healing, and supernatural-controlling spiritual folk tradition of the African American in the United States" (Hazzard-Donald 2013, 4).

In his 1977 seminal paper by the same title, Ralph R. Kuna calls Hoodoo, "the indigenous medicine and psychiatry of the black American." By my own analysis, these two experts aptly summed up the true essence of Hoodoo as it began in the United States.

The evolution of Hoodoo since the 1700s brought influences from France, Germany, Scotland, and Ireland, as well as from the local Native American tribes, changing how Hoodoo presents itself in our modern society. The most fundamental shift in the true nature of rootcrafting is the influence of what Katrina Hazzard-Donald calls "Marketeered Hoodoo," which occurred in post-Emancipation America and resulted in the form of Hoodoo we see today. Some researchers refer to this subsequent modernization of Hoodoo as "Urban Hoodoo."

Of all the changes Hoodoo experienced as it developed, the transition of the folk magic practice out of the hands of swampers, conjure doctors, and authentic rootworkers and into the mass-produced, factory generated, for-profit realm proved to be the most singularly destructive of any influence. Not only did it disrupt the reputation and integrity of Hoodoo, compromising its inherent authenticity, but it also served to inject a viciously competitive streak that still manifests in some of its most well-known contemporary workers.

————— 2 —————

Types of Practitioners

Despite the trauma and dehumanizing experience of being captured, transported, and sold as chattel, the enslaved Africans who developed what we now know as Hoodoo remembered and sustained many of the spiritual and healing traditions from Western and Central Africa. Those who held positions of power as healers and spiritual leaders in Africa often continued their practices once they settled onto the plantations of the American South, but took on new roles within the slave community as well. With the heirarchal structure dismantled by slavery, the healers and spiritual leaders were now forced to work side by side with the laborers, which reassigned their primary focus from spritual matters to issues of protection and survival.

Root Doctors

Root doctors healed using natural botanical products raised in fields, collected from the forests, and dug up from the swamps. There was no gender bias in the practice, so either men or women could be root doctors. The root doctor created tonics, poultices, tinctures, washes, disinfectants, and other applications of plant-based healing practices to treat the sick and injured slaves on the plantation.

In her 2002 book *Working Cures: Healing, Health, and Power on Southern Slave Plantations,* Sharla Fett says, "The midwife's touch, the conjurer's roots, and the herb doctor's pungent teas addressed the sufferer's pain as well as her or his standing within an extensive web of relationships. Seen in this light, slave doctoring, far from being a quaint and marginal folk practice, formed an integral part of the 'invisible institution' of slave religion."

As such, the root doctor was a source of treatment for physical maladies as well as mental and psychological issues. The root doctor sought not only the cure for the physical manifestation of illness or injury but also for the psychological dis-ease that created the problem.

In America, the word "disease" has become a throw-away term synonymous with "illness" or "sickness," to which we automatically assign a physical pathology. Throughout this book, you will see me write the word as "dis-ease," to distinguish a condition in which a person is not at ease for one reason or another. Dis-ease can occur on any level, including the physical, emotional, mental, sexual, psychic, or even social levels.

Root doctors understood that a disruption of the ease on any of these levels could potentially affect all the individual levels, so they addressed physical ailments of all kinds, as well as the social, spiritual, and mental ramifications of the condition, putting their practice leagues beyond the standards of traditional Western medicine either in their own time or even in our present time.

Conjure Doctors

Conjure doctors worked as spiritual consultants, using charms, tricks, jacks, and amulets as well as the power of breath, scripture, and prayer to treat their patients. Like the root doctor, they could be either male or female. Conjure doctors also worked as divinators and prognosticators and served as the embodiment of spirit within the African slave communities.

A frequent task for the conjure doctor was "uncrossing," or removing the hexes others placed upon their victims. The other side of this task was advising those who felt wronged in some fashion on how to curse or hex their offenders.

Two-Headed Doctors

Two-headed doctors worked in both areas of expertise, healing with herbs and roots as well as using charms, incantations, and touch to heal. Midwives within the slave culture are an excellent example of a two-headed doctor, managing the physical challenges of laboring women as well as employing charms, incantations, and other magical processes to decrease the pain of labor and the chance of complications occurring during childbirth.

—————— 3 ——————

History and Development of Hoodoo

Those who developed the processes of Hoodoo did not call what they did "magical," "supernatural," or even "Hoodoo." The exact origin of the word *Hoodoo* is a matter of heated debate. A primary talking point within that discussion is the lack of written evidence of the word *Hoodoo* in America until 1875, when we begin to find it used as both a noun and an adjective.

> *Hoodoo: (n) 1) The practice of Rootworking or Conjure 2) A spell—"She put a Hoodoo on you."*
> *Hoodoo: (adj) "That is a Hoodoo man."*

Some say the word is Scotch-Irish and comes from the phrase *Uath Dubh,* which is pronounced *"hooh dooh."* If this is so, it was not intended as a compliment, as *Uath Dubh* means "a dark entity" and might have been used in the same context that people of today would use the phrase "black magic," implying a fear and maligning of African spiritual and healing practices. There is no more concrete evidence of the word *Uath Dubh* used in Ireland or in America pertaining to the traditional African American folk magic systems than there is of "Hoodoo" itself as an identifying label. Those who adhere to the belief that *Hoodoo* derives purely from Scotch-Irish extraction appear to do so based more on what they have been told rather than on any form of solid and reputable evidence.

Others say the word comes from *Hudu*, which is a language spoken by the Ewe tribe in Togo and Ghana.

Some historians posit that the lack of written evidence of the word *Hoodoo* prior to 1875 is because African slaves were not allowed to read or write. Again, there is no strong documentation of this, only speculation. What is known is that those who developed the foundations of Hoodoo in the United States did not call their practices *Hoodoo* during its formative stages. Whether the term arose from within the culture or outside of it at some later point is ultimately unknown and unprovable.

Acclaimed African American author and Hoodoo initiate Zora Neale Hurston refers to it as "Hoodoo or 'Voodoo' as it is pronounced by the whites" in her book *Tell My Horse*. This statement is a nod to the theory that Caucasians created the word "Voodoo" as a derogatory reference to Hoodoo.

Many historians, as well as contemporary rootworkers, insist that they hold claim to the authentic extraction of the words *Voodoo* and *Hoodoo,* and engage in heated debate over their fiercely defended truths. When asked to produce legitimate documentation or evidence to support their beliefs, the answer is generally a guarded insistence that what they present is simply how it is.

More likely, the word's genesis is lost to the muddy waters of the cultures of the Scotch-Irish in the Appalachian and Ozark mountains and the African slaves of the American South, and neither employed the English language in its written form except on rare occasions. Most written accounts of life in the Antebellum South come from two categories of sources: journals, diaries, and household records kept by slave owners; and a gargantuan and problematic collection of charms and spells called *Hoodoo—Conjuration—Witchcraft—Rootwork* written by Harry Middleton Hyatt. Only recently have dedicated researchers explored beyond those sources to expand the authentic known history of African American healing and folk magic practices in the Antebellum and post-Emancipation years.

When a person explores the world of contemporary Hoodoo, what they find bears little resemblance to the healing and spiritual practices of the earliest slaves on American soil. The most reliable historical sources, however, suggest that the first practices of Hoodoo originated from the pre-capture memories of forcefully displaced people from different regions of Western and Central Africa.

What we do know is that although their beliefs differed in some ways, sufficient common ground existed for the captive slaves to create compatible spiritual and healing practices within the slave plantations of America. Over time, influences from the Scotch-Irish, the Pow-wows, the Native Americans, and the Louisiana French and Creole integrated into the healing tradition, as well as the syncretizing of Hoodoo onto the Protestant and Catholic Christian religions that came later.

Pennsylvania Dutch Pow-wow is a form of conjure practiced mostly in the Northern United States that derives from German origins. Although one might imagine it originates in Holland due to the identification as "Dutch," this is actually a culturally accepted misspelling of "Deutsch," meaning "German."

The post-World War emergence of a commercialized version of Rootworking finalized the amalgamation, creating a practice that is almost unrecognizable from its origins, and yet comprises what presents as Hoodoo/Rootworking today.

One of the primary attractions of Hoodoo in modern society is its effectiveness and its forgiving nature in terms of products used. Hoodoo recipes often do not include specific measurements or even a structured list of ingredients, relying instead on what the user has available in their cupboard. Hoodoo is, above all, versatile, which is part of the appeal.

The myriad arguments levied against modern Hoodoo are less about its efficacy and more focused on assertions of appropriation, observations on the deterioration of Hoodoo products available after the post-Emancipation African American migration north, and arguments over the finer points of practice and history. Few who have used Hoodoo techniques doubt its ability to get the job done.

Stages of Hoodoo Development

We can divide the development of Hoodoo into four trackable evolutionary phases largely instigated by the forced adaptation and cultural migration of the African Americans: Black Belt Hoodoo, Reconstruction era Hoodoo, post-Reconstruction era Hoodoo, and Marketeered Hoodoo.

Black Belt Hoodoo

"Black Belt Hoodoo" is a term coined by Katrina Hazzard-Donald that refers to the earliest form of Hoodoo practiced in the United States. Black Belt Hoodoo is the purest translation of the methods used in Central and Eastern Africa, established largely by those who experienced the spiritual and healing modalities of Central and Eastern Africa firsthand, and their next generation.

Black Belt Hoodoo distinguishes the folk magic practices developed on slave plantation from the New Orleans variety of Voodoo and Hoodoo. Although their origins are the same, the influence of Haitian Voodoo practitioners, Creole rootworkers, and Voodoo queens significantly changed the local presentation of Hoodoo in New Orleans from the practical methods used on the plantations, ultimately making it a unique practice. Another notable difference between the two is that because the New Orleans area is predominantly French, their Hoodoo syncretized onto Catholicism, while the Hoodoo in other southern regions of the United States became Protestant-based.

As the displaced Africans adapted their spiritual and healing work to the herbs, roots, and barks available in the American South, they also had to restructure their social classes and avocations within the oppressive environment they faced in slavery. Slave traders and slave owners ruthlessly dismantled families, villages, and hierarchies, necessitating that the spiritual and healing practices brought with them from Africa evolve to accommodate this vicious enforced cultural change.

Africans had to remember, sometimes over many years or through the eyes of previous generations, how they practiced in Africa and adapt those methods to their current conditions. Some primary components of their spirituality endured, while others dissolved in the face of slavery. In Africa, for instance, there was a strong emphasis on ancestral veneration. The breaking apart of families as slaves were bought, sold, and re-sold profoundly disrupted the ability to even know one's ancestors, much less honor them.

The conjure doctor, who was the revered priest of the village, now worked in the field with the other slaves, effectively shifting the dynamics of healing and spiritual practice between the patient and the healer. Continued oppression, born out of the fears of white slave owners, forbade or curtailed healing and religious gathering in some areas, forcing those practices underground.

While the Africans in America adjusted their spiritual practices to their new lives, subsequent waves of slaves arrived from Africa and brought with them perspectives closer to the authentic practices of their places of origin. This constant shifting and developing of the Hoodoo craft created a boiling pot of change and adaptation, responsive to the turnover of new arrivals.

The fluidity or stability of the slave population in a community influenced the degree of change in Hoodoo practices once they developed. How many slaves started out on a plantation, blending their remnant memories of practices from the homeland? How mixed was the community? Did the slaves on a specific plantation come from the same regions or vastly different areas of Africa, increasing the degree of cultural variances? How oppressive and restrictive were the slave owners? Did the slave owners allow or forbid spiritual expression and traditional healing practices? How large was the slave community and how fluid was the turnover?

Crops such as tobacco in Virginia required a small number of slaves to work the fields, but South Carolina's indigo and rice crops were more labor intensive, necessitating a larger community of workers. To what degree were the local Native Americans involved? Each of these components held greater or lesser influence on the development of spiritual and healing practices in a specific slave community.

Reconstruction-Era Hoodoo

Reconstruction era Hoodoo (1863–1877) once again shifted the Rootworking landscape through displacement of its practitioners and forced cultural and societal adaptation.

Although the Emancipation ended slavery, it did little to improve the plight of African Americans, and in fact, increased racial tensions in the South. Southern states, angry over the legal restrictions against slavery, instituted "Black Codes" that limited the rights of African Americans. It is important to remember that few slave owners considered slaves to be people and thought of them instead as property. Legislation forcing them to relinquish their purchased property created what they viewed as an unfair and unnecessary financial and practical hardship from both a business and a personal perspective.

The constitutional concept of "all men are created equal" did not apply to the freed slaves because most Americans did not consider them to be men, but instead, animals or property. Although technically freed, the emancipated African American could not vote, could not rent housing, could not have public social gatherings, and could not learn to read or write. In spite of those restrictions, they were required to have and—if questioned—*prove* employment of some type.

Prospects were limited, so many freed slaves remained at their current plantations or moved to nearby farms to work as sharecroppers. The increased persecution forced many African Americans to take a chance on migrating to the North where they could find factory jobs or journeying to the open frontiers of the West. Some went into Appalachia where there was little concept of slavery and land was easily available. As they once again moved away from familiar areas, many root-workers lost access to the roots, herbs, and barks they were accustomed to using for healing and Conjure work. Not all slaves knew Conjure techniques, and some relied on the healers within the slave community. The displacement and culture shock when moving to the northern states cannot be overstated.

At the same time, some of the true Black Belt rootworkers in the South set up shop offering their conjuring skills and services to African Americans who sought out authentic healing and spiritual assistance. Like their ancestors in Africa before them, they adopted eccentric styles of dress, acting as medicine men and women, and sustaining themselves independently through barter and the selling of their talents.

Although their daily lives shifted, the spiritual and healing needs of African Americans did not change significantly after Emancipation. Emphasis remained on the healing of injury and illness, the treatment of emotional maladies, establishing strong protection, bringing good fortune, and controlling wildlife and weather. For those freed slaves who migrated north, protection took on a different form and the concept of daily necessities expanded to the need for housing, jobs, and security.

Post-Reconstruction Hoodoo

The seventy years between the end of the Reconstruction era in 1887 and the end of World War II ushered in significant changes to the Hoodoo/Conjure landscape. The Great Migration resulted in Hoodoo practices from the deep South moving throughout different areas of the United States, blending with one another as rootworkers from different areas shared techniques.

In French-influenced Louisiana, Hoodoo syncretized with Catholicism through the use of the Blessed Mother and the saints as a pantheon of divine influences. Throughout other areas of the Southern United States, Hoodoo melded with the Protestant religions, and biblical figures such as Moses became primary influences. Both areas used the reading and application of psalms and other scriptures in their Conjure and healing practices. Although the syncretization of Hoodoo and Christianity began well before the Civil War, it was during the post-Reconstruction era that this union was cemented, ensuring the survival of Hoodoo.

The continued northward migration set the stage for the next developmental phase of Hoodoo, the Marketeered Era. Although this time would prove to be the most influential in creating the image of Hoodoo as it's presented in our modern times, there was still one unofficial battle that would create a significant change in the fundamental practice of Hoodoo.

The Relationship Between Hoodoo and Healing

The medical care of slaves was an economic dilemma for the slave owner. On one hand, a strong, healthy slave could do far more work than a sickly one, but on the other hand, white doctors were an expensive proposition, causing reluctance in slave owners to provide conventional medical care to the slave population. This issue led to the early establishment of African American healers as root doctors, conjure doctors, and two-headed doctors within the slave community, actively and openly treating the sick and injured.

Western medicine prior to the early 1900s was practiced from a dangerously ill-informed perspective and included the use of such substances as mercury, cocaine and opioid derivatives, arsenic, and chlorine. Although conventional medicine of the time was risky for the privileged white society, it was often deadly to the slave community.

To prove that the African American was a different species from the white slave owners, physicians performed barbaric experiments on slaves that they would never think to perform on white patients. In an article titled "SOUTHERN DISCOMFORT: Medical Exploitation on the Plantation," *New York Times* journalist Harriet A. Washington calls these facilities and practices "Medical Apartheid." The danger and resulting fear were sufficient enough that slaves often hid ailments from their owners, and instead sought healing from the community rootworkers to avoid a trip to the "slave hospital" and treatment by the white physicians.

As they began to see efficiency of the techniques used by the Black Belt healers, most slave owners quickly began to rely on the root doctors and conjure doctors to keep the slave population healthy. Although not considered a medical issue, Hoodoo healers managed not only injury and illness on the plantation, but also the care of pregnant and laboring women. With maternity care firmly in the hands of the African American midwives, root doctors and conjure doctors had easy access to materials such as cauls, umbilical cords, and placentas, which were used in some of their treatments.

The acumen and effectiveness of slave medical treatment led many wealthy white slave owners to seek out the advice and skills of African American healers for themselves and their families rather than incur the expense and inconvenience of sending for a white physician. Midwives and root doctors in the slave community sometimes treated an entire community of slaves as well as outsiders. This dealt a significant blow to the businesses of white physicians in the American South. It was no challenge at all for them to strike back and required only that they play on the natural fears of the white slave owners.

Although many slave owners trusted the African rootworkers with the medical care of their own families, the underlying fact was that within this dynamic, one party was the owner and the other party was owned, considered to be property rather than a human being. A few legitimate incidences of slaves poisoning their owners quickly tainted the trust slave owners had in African American healers and generated a wave of panic through white plantation owners. Slave owners faced the sudden awareness that any slave who held the balance of life and death, health and sickness, injury and recovery within their grasp had the power to inflict one just as easily as the other. The medical field was quick to capitalize on this fear and began pushing for restrictions on African healing practices.

Aggressive legislative action against slave healers solidified in 1748 when a Virginian law was passed forbidding any African American from preparing or administering medication of any kind. The law stated:

Whereas many negroes, under the pretence of practising physic, have prepared and exhibited poisonous medicines, by which many persons have been murdered, and others have languished under long and tedious indispositions, and it will be difficult to detect such pernicious and dangerous practices, if they should be permitted to exhibit any sort of medicine. Be it therefore enacted, by the authority aforesaid, that if any negroe, or other slave, shall prepare, exhibit, or administer any medicine whatsoever, he, or she do offending, shall be adjudged guilty of felony, and suffer death without the benefit of clergy.

Over the next hundred years, this law and many created in its image throughout other states forced Hoodoo healing far underground. In some instances, slaves could practice medicine "under the direction of their owner or master" and the punishment was reduced to lashings rather than death, so the slave owner did not lose their investment. Between 1748 and 1884, a total of 153 African Americans stood trial for using medicine illegally.

In absence of legal right to treat the sick and injured, Hoodoo rootworkers again adapted their practices to the existing paradigm. Root doctors who healed with herbs, roots, and other plant parts now hid their medicine in foods or treated their patients in secret to avoid discovery and prosecution. Greater reliance on conjure doctors (who healed with chants, charms, scripture, and breath) rather than root doctors (who administered herbal treatments more associated with medicine) developed out of this transition.

After the Emancipation and the subsequent realignment of African American social structures, many conjure doctors transitioned their Conjure practices into the worship services of black Protestant churches. This enabled them to work under the veil of religion, without interference from the legislation against medical practice.

One technique successfully integrated into church services was "ring shout," which was a form of traditional African Conjure involving percussion, dance, and an interactive shout and response dialogue between a leader and an assembled group. Linear pew arrangement within the church interrupted the classic circular formation of the ceremony, but again, conjure doctors and their followers adapted. The ring shout evolved into "shoutin'," a call and response praise technique that remains a mainstay of southern Protestant worship services even today.

Shoutin' is only one influence from the integration of conjure doctors into Christian worship services that continues into modern times. This is true not only in African American churches, but also in many Pentecostal and Baptist churches with predominately white congregations.

The unusual cadence of evangelical preaching in the South, practiced by ministers of color and Caucasian pastors alike, is quite distinctive and hearkens back to the affected "sacred voice" intonations of African Traditional Religions carried over into early Hoodoo practices. Full body immersion baptisms, snake handling, the laying on of hands for healing, and divine possession are also Hoodoo spiritual components that found their way into Protestant praise and worship, which is why you see these practices primarily in the South rather than throughout the country.

Although conjure doctors found their place within the ministry, the root doctors were not so fortunate. The fierce attack against African American healing practices instigated by the white medical field effectively ended lay midwifery and inflicted tremendous damage to the reputation, legitimacy, and efficacy of Hoodoo medical treatments. By the late 1800s, most root doctors slipped quietly back into underground practice, treating African Americans that sought them out for care.

The legislating and prosecution of medical services performed by African Americans resulted in most root doctors working on the down-low in such a way that only those who knew who to seek out for treatment were aware that authentic Hoodoo practices continued at all. Swampers still dug for roots and healers still harvested medicinal herbs, but combining those ingredients into healing tonics, tinctures, poultices, and other treatments constituted criminal activity. To avoid prosecution, root doctors became accessible only if you knew somebody who knew somebody.

Marketeered Hoodoo

Following World War I, the era of Marketeered Hoodoo began when Caucasian businesspeople stepped in and began mass marketing classic Hoodoo supplies, targeting this new demographic. Katrina Hazzard-Donald coined the phrase "Marketeered Hoodoo" to identify this developmental phase when Hoodoo left the hands of the swampers and rootworkers and entered the realm of commerce. Businesspeople, primarily Caucasian, moved into the field, and with little knowledge of the sacred processes behind the practice, exploited Hoodoo with the objective of profit rather than healing and protection.

In the late 1800s, traveling Wild West shows were a popular form of entertainment, featuring legendary performers such as Wild Bill Hickock, Calamity Jane, Annie Oakley, and Buffalo Bill. Presented as portable, pop-up vaudeville shows, some of these businesses traveled worldwide, performing even for European royalty.

An offshoot of this type of performance troupe production was what we now call the "snake oil salesman" or huckster, selling their own forms of Hoodoo and Hoodoo-type cures. These traveling vendors, usually Caucasian or worse, Caucasians in blackface, offered up amulets, mojo bags, tinctures, and other "tricks" without possessing the experience, background, or authenticity to back up what they sold.

Because they manufactured their wares with no knowledge of how they worked or the correct way to make them, quite frankly, their products did not work. For the huckster, the goal was not to provide an effective and viable medical treatment, but to whip the assembled crowd of customers into a buying frenzy, take their money, and then get out of town before the gullible buyer realized they had purchased fraudulent merchandise.

After the devastating effect of the white medical field's attack on rootworkers and the legislated racism inherent in the Black Codes, this association of Hoodoo products with charlatans, con men, and quacks was the final nail in the coffin for this vibrant and effective form of healing, greatly diminishing the level of respect and legitimacy it once possessed.

Throughout the Reconstruction era and the post-Reconstruction era, many freed slaves found life in the hostile South untenable and eventually moved north or west. Without the networked community ties to connect them with underground suppliers, they lacked the ingredients necessary to continue their healing and Conjure practices.

The first evidence of this appeared in drug stores in the northern states that began to openly carry manufactured Hoodoo products. Later, print media advertising appealed to the displaced African American community using fictive kin names and certain buzzwords to call attention to their product. Common phrasing looked like, "Brother, are you outside of your nature?" or "Sister, can you keep your man?"

Eager for familiar replications of products usually hand-made in the plantation communities of the South, African Americans in the North helped these new businesses to flourish. The compromise in the quality of marketed products was significant. Without the personalized service of the trained and experienced root doctors, the user was left to self-diagnose and work from memory to guess proper application and usage of the products. There was no longer any ritual associated with the creation of the product, nor any kind of ancestral or historical attachment. While they carried the same name as the authentic product, they did not use fresh or even "real" ingredients, so they were a weak imitation of their original form.

Often, the "recipes" for these products came from actual rootworkers who intentionally invented ingredients, omitted vital components, or deliberately misrepresented the instructions for preparation. To some degree, this was to undermine the efforts of those producing goods that were less than authentic, but also a natural reluctance to disclose Rootworking practices in the face of possible legal prosecution.

After World War II, candle shops came on the scene and quickly eclipsed drug stores as the most common source for Hoodoo products. Candles with classic Hoodoo verbiage such as "Bend Over," "Come to Me," and "Jinx Removing" grew in popularity, even though candles were not an authentic component of Black Belt Hoodoo. Candles were, in fact, rarely used in slave communities because they were quite expensive and not available anywhere except in the plantation manor. In addition to the sale of "fixed" candles, candle shops expanded their inventory to carry commercialized Hoodoo powders, oils, dirts, and dusts. After a brief surge of popularity, candle shops began to die out in the 1960s–1970s.

This final transition of Marketeered Hoodoo, along with the parallel development of a different kind of Hoodoo practice in Lousiana with French, Creole, and Haitian influences, created the version of Hoodoo that appears to us now.

Henry Middleton Hyatt

By the time Henry Middleton Hyatt collected material for his exhaustive five-volume, 4,766–page set, titled *Hoodoo— Conjuration—Witchcraft—Rootwork* in 1936–1948, the era of Marketeered Hoodoo was already well underway. His work is widely considered the most extensive collection of Hoodoo information ever published. Hyatt, an Anglican minister and amateur folklorist from Illinois, traveled through Alabama, Arkansas, Florida, Georgia, Illinois, Louisiana, Maryland, Mississippi, North Carolina, South Carolina, Tennessee, and Virginia interviewing self-identified rootworkers and Hoodoo practitioners.

Like nearly all historical documentation, his vast collection of information is a treasure to be sure, but it also reflects strong observational biases. Hyatt's previous work, *Folklore From Adams County Illinois,* received harsh criticism for its heavy-handed editing of the dialect of African Americans he interviewed.

Subsequently, in *Hoodoo—Conjuration—Witchcraft—Rootwork,* he transcribed his interviews phonetically, attempting to relay accurately and precisely what he was told. Of the 1,600 rootworkers interviewed, only one was white, despite evidence presented within his own text demonstrating his awareness that there were many white Hoodoo workers at the time. The fact that he was himself a white man interviewing African American Hoodoo workers caused many to speculate that the cultural divide between Hyatt and his subjects compromised the integrity of the interview process.

Racial tensions and legalized persecution were still fully in effect throughout the time of his interviews, and as a result, any legitimate rootworkers he quoted may not have been completely forthcoming with a Caucasian interviewer. Likewise, without the contextual experience to understand what he was hearing, we can reasonably speculate that plenty of opportunities existed for misinterpretation on his part.

The timing of his interviews is also problematic, as they occurred after Marketeered Hoodoo solidified as the dominant practice over Black Belt Hoodoo. This distanced many of his subjects from authentic Black Belt Hoodoo practices, which were now greatly diminished in favor of the commercialized processes and mostly lost to time and memory.

Equally concerning is Hyatt's lack of discrimination in his choice of interview subjects, such as his inclusion of those who told fanatical tales of "Hoodoo initiations" (which did not exist in the form he describes) and obviously fabricated ceremonies and spells. He presents these with equal legitimacy as the revelations that, to an experienced ear, are authentic and credible. This dissonance in the reliability of his subjects reflects poorly on the overall work and only adds to the growing impression at the time of Hoodoo as the repository for superstitious quacks.

For the reasons mentioned above, most rootworkers I know do not view Hyatt's work as a teaching guide or reputable resource for information, but more of a colloquial documentation of the time, conducted by a person outside of the community. The general consensus is that the observational bias, obvious cultural divide, and communication barriers created by dialectical differences sufficiently detract from the book's usability in any practical sense, although it is valued as a significant piece of history and an ambitious project.

4

New Orleans Voodoo

As a savvy person reads the history of Hoodoo presented in this book, from its Black Belt origins through many stages to its current incarnation, the obvious question is why the nexus of Voodoo and Hoodoo culture, New Orleans, has not yet warranted much of a mention.

This is one of the many areas where multiple truths exist, and again, I will attempt to provide the most universally accepted version of events mined from many reputable sources.

Throughout the American South, extending up the East Coast, Hoodoo practices developed based primarily on the information carried by the African diaspora. Knowledge of the Black Belt Hoodoo practices spread and cultural diffusion quickly resulted in overlapping from Native American and Scotch-Irish influences, as well as the Pow-wow practices of the Pennsylvania Dutch.

In Louisiana, however, there existed an entirely different set of societal factors that would result in a separate branch of Hoodoo that was the same and yet different from the blended practices found elsewhere throughout the American South.

It was in the midst of the slave trade years, in 1803, that the United States acquired the Lousiana territories from France. This accounted for a huge parcel of land, roughly more than one-quarter of the current continental United States, with the eastern boundary of that annexation defined by the Mississippi River. A good bit of this land remained unsettled, but the social hub of the area was New Orleans, Lousiana, which was home to a large French, Creole, and Cajun population. The Saint Domingue Revolution of 1791–1804 resulted in more than ten thousand Haitian slaves and non-slaves migrating to New Orleans. From 1830 through the early 1850s, interstate slave trade from the Atlantic states brought in slaves who originated specifically in Central Africa.

Two key factors in slavery practices dramatically changed how Hoodoo presented in Lousiana. One is that slaves originated from a more centralized area of Africa, primarily from the villages of Benin. Since many of the slaves came from the same area, the beliefs and practices they brought with them were similar, rather than the amalgam of practices more common on the plantations further east in the United States.

The second factor is that in Louisiana, slavers were legally required to sell families as a group, which helped to preserve hereditary traditions and ancestral veneration.

A cursory study of Hoodoo in Lousiana, and particularly in New Orleans, reveals that the word *Voodoo* is used more often than *Hoodoo*. Many who are new to the study believe Hoodoo and Voodoo to be the same. This is not the case at all, but is a source of confusion for people less familiar with the two practices.

Like Hoodoo, the spelling of "Voodoo" is one of the first hurdles. In Kreyol, the official language of Haiti, the spelling is "Vodou." In French, another predominant influence in Lousiana, the spelling is "Voudou." The Americanized version is "Voodoo." Any of the three is considered correct.

As you have seen through the previous discussion of Hoodoo's development in the United States, Hoodoo is a system of folk magic with roots in the African culture with an emphasis on healing and protection. Over time, the focus of the work done in Hoodoo changed as slavery ended and the needs of the practitioners shifted. Although Hoodoo is syncretized to Protestant Christianity, it is not itself a religion. It draws strongly from Christian mysticism, with elements of ceremonial magic, as well as components of African, European, and Native American folk magic.

Voodoo, on the other hand, is a religion in which practitioners venerate and serve the Lwa (*L'wah*), also spelled Loa (*Lo-ah*), which are the spirits of Haitian Vodou and Lousiana Voodoo. Each of the Lwa has their own personality, sacred dances, rituals, symbols, songs, and requirements of those in service to them. Unlike Hoodoo, which is set up as a practical working system to manage problems as they occur, New

Orleans Voodoo has a greater emphasis on spirituality, which resulted in altars, mass rituals, and offerings to the Lwa.

New Orleans birthed expressive and prominent Voodoo queens and priests, neither of which was a component of the Black Belt Hoodoo community. The most famous of these were Marie Laveau, Doctor John, and Doctor Buzzard. Sanité DeDe, Marie Saloppe, Bayou John, and other strong leaders also held public gatherings on Dumaine Street and in Congo Square, complete with drumming, dancing, trancework, singing, ancestor veneration, and celebration.

Free people of color rose to greater affluence in New Orleans and Lousiana than in other parts of the Southern United States. It was not unusual for well-to-do people of any race to seek out the Voodoo leaders for their advice and assistance. The use of Hoodoo techniques was often part of this type of practice.

Throughout the nineteenth century, while Black Belt practices suffered ongoing compromises to the integrity of its primary structure, as described in previous chapters of this book, New Orleans Voodoo thrived and experienced its golden age. Far from eschewing commercialization, New Orleans practitioners embraced it and openly marketed magical services, so that Voodoo became synonymous with the city and a central component of its identity, much like jazz music and French/Creole cuisine.

Because of how similar "Hoodoo" sounds to "Voodoo" and the misrepresentations propagated by Hollywood and those wishing to lump together all magical paths with

African roots, the two systems are frequently confused with one another. The fact that many Voodoo practitioners also are rootworkers contributes to the confusion for those outside the practice.

Ultimately, the Hoodoo that developed in Louisiana included Haitian, French, Cajun, Spanish, and Louisiana Creole influences layered onto the African folk magic structure. Specifically, the use of gris-gris (a small bag of magical items devoted to a specific cause); perfumed waters such as Florida Water; traditional oils such as VanVan, Cleo May, and Come to Me; and the use of cloth poppets rather than doll effigies made from sticks are the signatures of European influence.

5

Basic Beliefs of Hoodoo

With such a wide array of formative factors, as well as the eventual removal of the spiritual aspects of authentic Black Belt Hoodoo, we encounter a significant challenge when attempting to nail down any sort of common beliefs.

Slave communities on plantations consisted of people originating from many different areas of Africa, all with their own indigenous beliefs. Beneath the outward differences of practice were underlying culturospiritual commonalities that allowed for interconnection and the formation of a new type of healing and Conjure built upon the authentic African practices. Among those common beliefs were a reverence for family connections and ancestral wisdom, the veneration of elders, the communal nurturing of children, ritual water immersion for spiritual cleansing and transition, a respect for nature, and the use of ritual animal sacrifice. By finding their common ground, they also found their strength, and from that very genesis, the practices of Hoodoo that would ultimately endure began to grow.

In the modern presentation of Hoodoo, individual theologies shift not only from one branch of practice to the next, but from one rootworker to the next. The absence of spiritual attachment to the magical processes of Hoodoo opens the door for each worker to connect with their own image of the Divine and to layer that onto the practical applications.

Syncretization of Catholic and Protestant Christianity onto African traditional religious beliefs was a vital step in the sustainability of Hoodoo. The Christian Church was sufficiently aggressive that had the practices not incorporated the veneration of Catholic saints and the use of Protestant praise modalities, Hoodoo would not likely have survived.

The assignment of Catholic saints and biblical figures such as Moses and Solomon gave Hoodoo a strong pantheon of divine intercessors that legitimized practice within a predominantly Christian culture. Author and journalist Zora Neale Hurston said, "Moses was the finest Hoodoo man in the world" (Hurston 2009, 114), and "All hold that the Bible is the great conjure book in the world" (Hurston 2008, 280). The miracles Moses channeled from God to free the slaves of Egypt resonated strongly with the African American slaves and became a representation of Hoodoo's supernatural power.

Not only are scriptures used as incantations, but the Bible itself is revered as a magical talisman and can be carried for protection or left open to specific scriptures used for Conjure work. Often in the latter use, the Bible is positioned to face a compass direction sympathetic to the effect the practitioner wishes to create.

The foundation of Hoodoo remains primarily Christian, either Catholic or Protestant. Many rootworkers hotly protest the inclusion of non-Christian practitioners such as Wiccans and others in the Pagan world who practice Hoodoo.

Hedge Witches, Wiccans, and other Pagans who participate in spellwork and focused energy manifestation techniques often embrace Hoodoo, drawn to its simple processes, easily obtainable tools, and the similarity of healing and magical techniques when compared to other forms of folk magic. The Celtic Cunning People, for instance, could study the practice of Black Belt Hoodoo healing and conjuring and immediately feel at home, quickly understanding the terminology, processes, and applications. Someone who works with poppets finds Voodoo dolls and Hoodoo doll babies familiar and has a basic idea of how to use them. The crossroads concept, a powerful component of Hoodoo work, is the sacred domain of the Greek Goddess Hecate, so any follower of Hecate will immediately relate to the veneration of the crossroads and the magic created there.

Relatability is the strongest pull of Hoodoo, and it has within it components familiar to magical people from multiple paths. Many feel that their previous magical experience led them to choose Hoodoo as their preferred path, for the ability to blend all the techniques they previously learned into a single practice.

One aspect of Hoodoo that has not changed since the Black Belt days is the use of herbs, stones, resins, roots, animal body parts, and body fluids such as semen, menstrual blood, urine, and saliva. Skin, hair, and nail trimmings also bind the magical work to a party involved with the magical process.

The closer to its natural state, the stronger the energy in an herb, root, or blossom. Rosemary that you grow, cultivate, harvest, dry, and store yourself has a stronger energy pattern than a container of rosemary purchased at the local grocery store. The grocery store version will fulfill the needs of the magical work, but the materials created by the hand of the rootworker always carry a bigger magical punch. Most Hoodoo practitioners use dried versions of their natural ingredients for the convenient storage.

There is almost no concept you can point to and say "All rootworkers believe this" or "All Hoodoo practitioners believe that." Philosophies within Hoodoo are as varied as those who practice it. It is the methodology that is similar, rather than any structured belief system. Even in practical application, traditions vary significantly according to how the person was taught or under what rootworker they apprenticed.

The one prevailing idea that I see manifested in most rootworkers I know is one of personal accountability. Most Hoodoo workers I know embrace the belief that we all make choices, magically and mundanely, and if we do not achieve the desired outcome or worse, if we manifest an undesired outcome, it is up to us and no one else to extricate ourselves and thereby to create a different outcome. There is also no one to blame or praise but ourselves for what we manifest in our lives. No one will take care of us other than ourselves and our own tribe, familial or chosen. We must own both our victories and our mistakes in life and do whatever it takes to heal what we can, accept and release what we cannot, atone where we should, and forever work to improve ourselves, our lives, and our contribution to the human species. We must rise out of any adversity. We must adapt and evolve as life demands. We must accept the new while honoring the past.

A culture and practice that fails to adapt to the surrounding realities will not survive, much less thrive. The same can be said about individuals. The ability of Hoodoo to shift and adapt despite oppressive and forceful restructuring is a testimony to the devotion and perseverance of those who believed in it and wanted it in their lives. It is both our responsibility and our privilege to carry forward the heart of Rootworking, honoring the past and embracing the future, with the same determination and persistence demonstrated by those who went before us.

——— 6 ———
Hoodoo/Conjure/ Rootwork Today

The foundation of Black Belt Hoodoo practices that developed from the memories of captured slaves created the bedrock for spiritual and healing practices in the African American plantation communities. It endured despite untenably oppressive conditions and defied aggressive legislation intended to entirely eradicate it. Its ability to adapt to ongoing transition accounts for its very survival. The American South availed itself of every opportunity to destroy the African Traditional Religions (ATR) and the African healing and spiritual traditions, and yet, Hoodoo prevailed.

For centuries, the history of Hoodoo and Voodoo were presented primarily through the words of white slave owners, filtered through a perspective of privilege. Cultural boundaries inhibited accurate and cohesive understanding of practices that ran much deeper than superstition and lore.

In recent years, a more authentic representation of the developmental states of Hoodoo through the centuries emerged, entirely due to the hard work of researchers who dug deep into historical records to track the impact of enforced cultural change on the magical practices in the United States. Most of what we know comes from the efforts of people like Zora Neale Hurston, Albert J. Rabateau, Yvonne P. Chireau, and Katrina Hazzard-Donald.

Anthropologist, journalist, and novelist Zora Neale Hurston wrote a series of fictional books and folklore collections that illustrated life during various phases of the development of Voodoo and Hoodoo. *Mules and Men* (1935), *Their Eyes Were Watching God* (1937), and *Moses, Man of the Mountain* (1939) are considered her greatest works, as well as her classic study of Voodoo in Haiti and Jamaica, *Tell My Horse* (1938).

Albert J. Raboteau wrote the book *Slave Religion: The "Invisible Institution" in the Antebellum South,* which was a seminal study of slavery that helped to launch the Black Studies Movement of the 1970s.

Yvonne P. Chireau wrote *Black Magic: Religion and the African American Conjuring Tradition*, an extensive and frank study of Conjure from the slavery period through the twentieth century. Her analysis of the history of Hoodoo speaks strongly to how magical practice informed the spirituality and healing modalities of Africans in the American South.

Katrina Hazzard-Donald wrote *Mojo Workin'*, which is arguably the consummate academic work on the origins and development of Hoodoo in the African diaspora. Although her extensive work in the research of Black Belt Hoodoo practices in America is sometimes criticized as largely speculative and without substantiation, I would argue that the lack of credible documentation itself necessitates a speculative approach. The blanks she fills in, based partially on her background in authentic African music, provide a strong foundation for the expansion of our working knowledge of Hoodoo history in America.

In the modern world of Hoodoo, our public rootworkers commonly present themselves as authors, bloggers, video-bloggers, teachers, and business owners. In comparison to Granny Magic and Brujería, the Hoodoo community has many public experts and elders, all of whom have their own stories and truths. Without working hard to think about it, I can name Starr Casas, Carolina Dean, Cat Yronwode, the late Dr. E. (Eddy Gutierrez), Professor Charles Porterfield, Orion Foxwood, Talia Felix, Denise Alvarado, Dorothy Morrison, Chief Amachi, Dr. Christos Kioni, Stephanie Rose Bird, and Deacon Millett as well-known personalities in the field. Each one of these people contributed on a grand scale to the aggregate knowledge of Hoodoo, and on a smaller scale, to my own education and Hoodoo practice.

Unlike Granny Magic and Brujería, Hoodoo in its current incarnation carries with it an underlying animosity that is palpable upon even a cursory exploration through online resources. If we follow the notion that the seed creating a movement informs the totality of its progress, Hoodoo developed out of the unjust and unearned dominance of one culture over another. This oppression not only continues through the current presentation of Hoodoo, but shaped it, forcing adaptation through an ongoing series of injustices.

When you look at photos of these famous rootworkers, all of whom are expertly qualified practitioners and teachers, you can see where accusations of appropriation come into play. Of those thirteen well-known practitioners who I listed without effort or research, only three of them—Stephanie Rose Bird, Chief Amachi, and Dr. Kioni—are visually identifiable as African American. Of course, most people know and understand that how a person looks does not always reflect their cultural heritage or genealogy, and yet, many of the attacks leveled from a racial perspective are directed at the marketing images of these rootworkers who appear to be Caucasian.

There is an underlying current, sometimes subtle and sometimes loud and angry, that while Hoodoo is an African American practice, the people who are making money from it are, on initial visual identification at least, white. My own mentors, Hexeba Theaux and Maya Grey, both excellent rootworkers and extremely knowledgeable about the history of Hoodoo, are Caucasian. Cat Yronwode, arguably the most influential living person in commercialized Hoodoo, is a Jewish woman.

A Community Divided

The racial component is only one point of division within the Hoodoo community. Many African American practitioners feel non-African American rootworkers are guilty of appropriation of a magical practice to which they are not entitled and that this is disrespectful to their culture. There is the pervasive infusion of the mindset of "You took everything from us; must you now claim this as well?" Some Hoodoo practitioners with direct historical lineage to Black Belt Hoodoo claim that without the genealogical and cultural context to adequately relate to the true origins of the practice, the spiritual aspect of the work is compromised.

Rootworkers specifically from the Cajun Bayou and New Orleans-based tradition of Hoodoo shoot back that the European people had just as much influence on the tradition as the Africans, and therefore claim ancestral entitlement to practice Hoodoo. Others insist that Hoodoo is primarily a Scottish and Pictish practice with only minimal African influence. Many Christian rootworkers insist that Pagan and non-denominational people have no right to claim that what they do is anything remotely close to Hoodoo, even if they use traditional Hoodoo recipes and techniques.

Some even go as far as to say that certain roots or recipes will not work for non-Christian or non-African American practitioners. I have personally found this not to be the case and feel qualified to comment since I am neither Christian nor African American, so it becomes less an issue of "Will the techniques and tools work?" and more of a question of the ethics of cultural and magical appropriation.

Maya Grey addresses the subject quite well when she says this:

> In terms of "not everyone can practice Hoodoo," it may simply be that some folks are just not gifted for this kind of work. It is like anything else. Some may have a proclivity for football or violin and others do not. One may try to learn any of these skills, but it may take years of grinding work and come less easily for some than for others. In my experience, you need to know yourself, have a strong will and sense of self and be beloved of the Spirits to get results.
>
> Practicing Hoodoo is about getting results whether they be for positive or negative outcomes for yourself and clients. If you are not getting results (not "feelings" but actual quantifiable results), something is not working, and you must explore why. Delve deeper. Study more. Practice more. Observe.
>
> Hoodoo is about solving the problems of life. It is street magic, like getting people out of prison, making debt disappear, finding love or sex, and hurting or neutralizing your enemies. These are real life gritty situations where your hands and feet are in mud, bone, smoke, and whiskey.

Put yourself in the shoes of a desperate client. Would you go to a lawyer, doctor, counselor if they never won, cured, or helped anyone? Nah, me neither.

Hoodoo was born of oppression, and in many ways, I think that it is relevant now more than ever. We are living in vastly uncertain times where racism is rearing its ugly head trying to pull back all our hard-fought gains. We live in a world where income and social inequality are on the lips of all.

Hoodoo can slip through the cracks, make the paperwork fail or succeed, help the innocent to be freed and the evil to be punished. What is a locked door to a spirit of the dead? Hoodoo is unseen and goes where it will.

Hoodoo is the working man and woman's system of magic. It is the magic of the oppressed and it is there to help even the playing field. It can and does work. I have seen it, I lived it, I have worked it. Remember, though, that the work you do in Hoodoo must be justified by the spirits themselves. This is the path of the spiritual worker in Hoodoo: part streetwise mystic, part seer, and part herbalist. The good rootworker is clever, quick on their feet, and gets the job done with what is on hand—and I believe we are going to need more of them in the days ahead.

Most rootworkers I know personally understand and respect why others feel the way they do, but choose to instead cite the adaptive spirit of Hoodoo as an ever-evolving practice. This mindset calls for the inclusion of all rootworkers who experience a calling and embrace the heart of Rootwork.

Hoodoo worker and political activist, Channyn Lynne Parker says, "Hoodoo's origins are rooted in the slaves of the African Diaspora, but what we know now as Hoodoo, is Pow-wow, Native American, and a gumbo of other magic as well. I just think that this is all being so over complicated."

As a woman of color with a strong foundation in ancestral practice, the subject is close to Parker's heart and her history. She goes on to say:

The thing is that at some point, as people of the African Diaspora, we have got to make peace and reconcile with those more complicated pieces of our bloodline. We must keep in mind that it is the "right now" in the magic that IS Hoodoo and "right nows" change ... the usage and the means of Hoodoo evolve with the climate and the times that we are living in and currently facing.

On the whole, the practice of Hoodoo has become that of veneration; a remembrance of our ancestors' bare bones survival. It's not glitz, glam, and ritualistic. It speaks to the "kitchen magician" in us all. If you put your ears to the belly of Hoodoo, you will hear the sigh of Protestants, tired of the pretention of the Catholic Church. You'll hear the slave mother putting all her heart and soul into the creation of a charm she'll hope will ward off a lusty overseer tonight. You'll hear Granny in Appalachia, rubbing a concoction of salve onto the chest of her son, fearful that she'll lose yet another child to sickness. In short, you will hear the underpinnings of humanity in Hoodoo, the common thread of wanting to survive that is in us all. I hear them all … I hear their mistakes, their pain, their joys. I can't hate any of the contributors to my existence, by fair or by foul. Without them, there would be no me.

Even within the cliques of modern Hoodoo practice, people are on the attack. A cursory search of Hoodoo blogs online will show many posts of rootworkers arguing that this person is not legitimate because of this reason, or that person is not entitled to practice for that reason. Full blog posts consist of authors defending themselves against these attacks with long pedigrees presented to explain why their participation in Hoodoo is valid. In short, tremendous energy is invested into the arguments of who is and is not a legitimate worker, almost to the point of surpassing the energy invested into the craft of Hoodoo itself.

I asked Maya Grey, the rootworker I quoted earlier in this chapter, why this was the case, and she proposed a reason I had not previously considered, which was that Hoodoo was one of the first magical paths to commercialize in such a way that practitioners were paid to work magic for others. This immediately created the competitive field that persists among rootworkers to this day. In such a field, some feel that the only way to get ahead is to discredit the competition. While this may not be the sole reason for divisiveness in the Hoodoo community, it is most certainly a factor.

Truly, however, Hoodoo in American practice was born out of turmoil and oppression, which remained so ingrained for centuries. As such, it is difficult to imagine that it could become a path of harmony and accord in such a short time, and indeed, it did not. Taken on its own merits, the techniques specific to Hoodoo bring strong results, and most rootworkers I know are quite satisfied with their chosen magical path. As a collective community, however, it is every bit as jagged and polarized as the environment from which it was birthed.

The Rebirth of Hoodoo Practice

The United States experienced a renewed interest in Hoodoo within the past few years. The appeal of a very basic system of magic designed to overcome adversity draws quite a crowd during times of poverty and loss of hope. Direct accountability for one's own actions becomes attractive to those who feel they cannot trust others around them to be accountable.

Throughout the world, rootworkers use Hoodoo practices independently of any spiritual practice, while others layer their own belief system onto a Hoodoo framework. Some Hoodoo practitioners who vehemently insist that *only* Christian people who accept the Bible as their spiritual doctrine may practice Hoodoo or identify as a rootworker find this offensive.

Currently, the strongest points of contention among Hoodoo practitioners involve the precise details of its history and development, who has a right to practice it, and what constitutes a "legitimate" rootworker. These issues are hotly debated topics within the Hoodoo community and sometimes result in vicious conflict.

In the contemporary New Orleans area, the role of the two-headed doctor who practiced as both a conjure doctor and a root doctor is now the domain of the "treater," or "traiteur" in Cajun/Creole. These healers still use the power of scripture, voice, breath, and herbs, although most traiteurs adamantly deny any magical component to their practice or any affiliation with Hoodoo or Rootworking. Most identify as Christian and heal using sacred knots, string work, herbal remedies, charms, and prayer. By tradition, a traiteur never asks for or accepts payment for their work and the client must ask them to assist rather than the traiteur offering of their own accord. Most specialize in a particular field of healing, such as skin disorders; tooth pain; eyes, nose, and ears; tumors; internal organs, or bleeding.

Although in its current incarnation Hoodoo is not a religious practice itself, to say that Rootworking is devoid of spirituality oversimplifies the practice. Often, this perspective is presented as a means of distancing Hoodoo, seen as a harmless folk magic practice, from Voodoo, which society views as more sinister and suspicious. This is of the same ilk as, "Oh, you're a *Wiccan*, not an actual *Witch*." Just as the term *Wiccan* mollifies the fears of a skeptical public as far as

Witches are concerned, Hoodoo practice seems benign, provided it remains unaffiliated with Voodoo.

This separation between the secular and spiritual practices to all appearances began with the medical laws enacted against the African American healers and continued through the marketeering phase, finding completion around the turn of the twentieth century. The removal of spiritual involvement from Hoodoo persists. In modern practice, only the natural expressions of the Divine used in the Rootwork bring a spiritual component to the process, although individual Hoodoo practitioners may imbue their own spiritual process onto the work.

Regardless of why or how the two paths parted, at this stage of evolution, Hoodoo serves most practicing rootworkers as an expression of self-empowered, effective, nature-based folk magic and Conjure practice. It is a call to the grassroots (quite literally in this case) of magic. There is nothing more basic than blending herbs, roots, essential oils, bones, dirt, vinegar, body effluvia, and other natural products into a traditional recipe with the specific purpose of helping another person to heal from trauma, abuse, or misfortune.

My own call to Hoodoo/Conjure/Rootwork was something I could not ignore if I tried, which I did at first. It was pervasive and profound, presenting itself repeatedly and on a regular basis, each time with increasing insistence that it was what I meant to do. Ultimately, I followed it, studied extensively on my own, and then reached out to two local teachers who fine-tuned my education.

Most rootworkers I know practice in the same way that I do. They handmake Hoodoo products, seeking out the most authentic and natural recipes and ingredients available, usually growing their own herbs, digging up their own roots, and otherwise personally collecting natural materials for use. They then offer the products they create for the client to use themselves, which carries its own level of magical power layered onto the efforts of the rootworker. Alternatively, the client may choose to procure the further services of the rootworker and have them perform the magical work on their behalf.

This arrangement dates to the earlier days of Hoodoo, when rootworkers such as Dr. Buzzard would "chew the root" for a client who expected no justice in the outcome of their court case. He would sit in the courtroom during the proceedings while chewing on Low John (galangal) root.

Marie Laveau, who, along with other Voodoo queens, often did the actual Rootwork on behalf of their clients, is said to have prayed for a client for hours while holding three guinea peppers in her mouth. She then placed the peppers near the judge's seat and the client was set free. Marie allegedly received a house in payment for these services.

Most rootworkers charge only a modest fee for their products and services, viewing their craft as a mission to their community rather than a path to riches. Unfortunately, those who do take untoward advantage of people in need are often the loudest and most visible faces of modern Hoodoo. A client recently contacted me by email saying that she had paid a

Hoodoo priest more than eight thousand dollars to win back the love of her ex-fiancé. When she saw no results after her investment, the Hoodoo priest explained to her that her fiancé had left her because of an ancestral curse upon her that he would remove—you guessed it—for a few thousand more dollars, as well as sixteen pieces of underwear and forty-seven red candles, which she was to bring to him in a cemetery. At this point, she began to suspect the man was a fraud and contacted me to ask my opinion after viewing some of my YouTube video classes.

These types of charlatans are the modern-day equivalent of those marketeering age snake oil peddlers who took advantage of the client, then disappeared into the night. Fortunately, most rootworkers are honest, experienced people who approach Hoodoo with the belief that they are working in strong conjunction with nature toward the best possible outcome.

The Return to the Root

The trend of "returning to the root" grew in popularity over the past several years after decades of derision and dismissal of the path, either from fear or skepticism. Why is it so popular now? We find the answer in our current economic turndown. When times are tough for many in our society, those who practice magic are inevitably affected as well, and those who do not normally seek supernatural modalities to solve their problems start to explore non-traditional options. When people feel disempowered or disadvantaged in their own lives, they seek new ways to resolve crisis and undesired life conditions.

Hoodoo does not require extensive formal instruction, expensive tools or ingredients, and it is quite effective. When life is good and things go the way we expect or want them to, there is no great desire to create change. On the contrary, most people will avoid "rocking the boat" and actively work to maintain the status quo. When we suffer setback after setback and have difficulty creating or maintaining the life we want, many of us feel ready to try something different.

Hoodoo Uses Natural Ingredients that Are Easily Obtained

During times of financial hardship, expensive ceremonial tools and robes go off the radar and people look for answers to their problems that do not involve a significant financial investment. Because Hoodoo originated using the most basic supplies available, it is quite forgiving in terms of ingredients. Look at any legitimate Hoodoo "cookbook" and you will notice two things right away. One is that there are no measurements offered, no "half a teaspoon of this" or "four grams of that." The rootworker adds the amount of each ingredient that feels and smells right to them.

Next, you will see that there is a very long list of ingredients for nearly every recipe, usually with the directions to "pick six of these" or something similar. Hoodoo is quite literally about what you have on hand in your cupboard or what you can easily acquire. Four Thieves Vinegar, for instance, is a disinfectant that works the same way on your home that white sage does on the air around you. It purifies in the same fashion, but works on the structure of the home rather than the air. Every bottle of Four Thieves Vinegar should have a piece of garlic in it. Beyond that, you add three more "thieves" from a list of twenty or so ingredient options, including but not limited to lavender, rue, nutmeg, camphor, or sweet flag. Any will work just fine. For one batch of Four Thieves, you might use wormwood, mint, and sage. For another, cinnamon, clove, and rosemary. If you have that bit of garlic in there, it will dance just fine with any of the other ingredients on the list. This versatility is the beauty and simplicity of Hoodoo.

You will notice that many of the ingredients listed to make Four Thieves Vinegar are common kitchen herbs. We add these to a red wine vinegar base, leading one of my mentors, Hexeba Theaux, owner of Cajun Conjure, to say, "It might smell like meat marinade, but please *don't eat the Hoodoo!*"

She maintains that items created for magical use take on a separate function and form than the same items used in the exact same combinations for culinary or other mundane purposes. I tend to agree with this conclusion and strongly suggest that when you make your own concoctions and decoctions, *don't eat the Hoodoo!* Hexeba also scoffs when her students expect a fragrant, pleasant product from their Hoodoo efforts. She laughs and says, "Honey, this ain't aromatherapy."

Hoodoo Tailors Each Process to the Individual Client/User

One of the greatest criticisms of Marketeered Hoodoo was that the commercialization and mass production removed the personalized spirit from the magical process. The conscientious rootworker now either makes their own products or purchases them from a trusted Hoodoo shop, supplier, or worker. Hoodoo products are not at all difficult to make, and creating them for yourself or those close to you intimately connects the rootworker and the client with the process. As you make the product, you know who will use it and how they will use it, which informs the magical process. This allows your vision for the outcome to permeate the work.

Although the forgiving aspect of Hoodoo affords an easy immersion for most new rootworkers, it is advisable to find a teacher who can help with the finer points and guide the novice as they learn.

As in the past, a primary benefit to working with a Hoodoo practitioner is their availability. Most adepts offer classes to share their knowledge and also provide their services to the community at large. As Hexeba says, "Root doctors: we make house calls."

Information Is Readily Available

As previously stated in this book, the Hoodoo community is divisive and highly defensive of their perceived truths, but is also the most prevalent of the three folk magic paths this book will discuss, in terms of the availability of information.

Fortunately, the world wide web gives everyone a voice, and plenty of free information is available if you know how to use a search engine. It is easy to shop around and look for Hoodoo niches that feel organic and right to you. Research extensively and find what "traditional" recipes for Hoodoo compounds, oils, powders, washes, and other products seem authentic and which ones feel sketchy.

Prepare to spend some time dropping into the proverbial rabbit hole when researching Hoodoo information online. Online booksellers offer huge libraries of information, and YouTube is home to literally hundreds or even thousands of instructional videos from every niche and theological perspective of Hoodoo.

If your interest in Hoodoo leads you to a deeper exploration of the subject, tune in to your spirit and trust your instincts. See what feels authentic to you and fully engage your spirit in the conversation. You will find the information that is right for you, and if you tune in, you will know instinctively what to avoid.

Hoodoo Fosters Accountability

Hoodoo empowers the client and the worker to know that both help and answers are available. It teaches those who use it to refuse to be a victim and to take action, regardless of their circumstances. When people feel helpless, there is nothing more empowering than to know that they can personally do something to create change. A primary focus of Hoodoo is on keeping your own side of the street clean and living a good life, but also that you must not hesitate to take action if another person aggresses against you or compromises your quality of life in a way that is intolerable. Hoodoo tells you that regardless of the oppression or challenges you face, you do not have to take it lying down. You can harness the energy of nature, direct the energy of God, and infuse your own inherent energy into the process of finding and enacting a reasonable solution. One of the most fulfilling aspects of my job is when someone humbles themselves to contact me as their last resort for problem solving, then feels positive and confident once we have worked together to establish a worakble and actionable plan to resolve their crisis.

Hoodoo Works

Hoodoo gets results. The lack of ceremony, circle casting, quarter calls, and elaborate invocations in favor of scripture and simple ingredients does not diminish the inherent power of Rootworking. It is a visceral and effective magical process that withstood the greatest oppression any culture can imagine and yet remains a force that creates positive change on an ongoing basis.

Contemporary rootworkers are often educated, professional people who began as apprentices and branched out on their own as their skills developed. Many incorporate the tarot or other divinatory systems and oracles into their practice for guidance. Their study is ongoing and adaptive, much as Hoodoo itself is adaptive. Although commercialized Hoodoo is still prominent, many rootworkers accept word-of-mouth referrals and do their work without involving accolades, fanfare, or ego.

Reconstructionists of the old ways seek to unearth as many of the traditional recipes as possible and yes, there are a few families with ties going all the way back to the Black Belt Hoodoo times who passed vital information through subsequent generations, preserving the healing and spiritual techniques developed by slaves on southern plantations. Authentic Black Belt practice in its truest sense, however, is virtually nonexistent.

Many valuable practices fell victim to the ongoing enforced changes throughout the centuries of Hoodoo development. Most of what we know is left to speculation and assumptions, and, to our advantage, those publishing their ideas do so from an increasingly educated and open-minded perspective.

The many stages of Hoodoo's development resulted in the effective and vibrant path that many rootworkers now employ to help others and to help themselves. In spite of or because of the trauma of slavery, the Africans brought to this country clung fiercely to their cultural beliefs of healing, honoring their ancestral dead, and working with the forces of nature. Because of their tenacity and ability to adapt their practices to ongoing societal turmoil, Hoodoo refused to be crushed into the dirt of time, despite centuries of oppression. Instead, it picked up that dirt and made a spell out of it. It endured. And although it now presents in a different package than it did at its beginning, it remains a force for good in an unsure world.

7

Hoodoo Charms
and Spells

A common thread with Granny Magic, Hoodoo, and the folk magic of Mexican origins is that magic is done in the moment to address a specific need and typically uses easily obtained materials. Often, the practitioner chooses from any number of spell components, based on what they have available at the time. The role of the rootworker is to know the magical properties of a multitude of herbs, stones, roots, and human or animal biological products and combine them in a particular way to achieve the desired outcome. There are countless Hoodoo spells, chants, tricks, and incantations for almost any spiritual, physical, emotional, or social ailment. These are just a few.

The Nature Sack

One of the most famous authentic Hoodoo tricks is the nature sack. Many people mispronounce this as a "nation sack." The reason for the confusion is clear. At their services, Protestant ministers passed around a "donation sack" for monetary offerings. To mock the ministers, prostitutes of the time tied a drawstring purse to their thigh to hold their earnings and called it their 'nation sack.

When Henry Middleton Hyatt phonetically transcribed his interviews, rootworkers spoke of the nature sack and pronounced it "naitcha" sack, which many white people took to mean "nation," knowing of the 'nation sacks carried by the prostitutes and confusing the terms.

The true focus of the nature sack is to control a man's "nature," which is his ability to achieve an erection. Women did so to keep their partner from wandering, thereby binding him to have intimacies only with her. The cord of the nature sack was tied by the female during the peak of the sex act and she had to be very careful to do so without the man's knowledge, because men were understandably hostile to the idea of any woman holding such power over them.

Brick Dust

One of the best-known Hoodoo practices is the use of brick dust to create protective boundaries, made popular in the 2005 film *The Skeleton Key*, starring Kate Hudson. Brick dust is a highly effective boundary, although other less-expensive products such as sea salt and cascarilla (finely ground egg-shells) work very well.

My shop was in a highly trafficked area and few people come to that location looking for magical items. It sat along-side a farmer's market with great deals on produce and many swap meet-type booths. To screen my customers and make sure no one got into the shop who was not supposed to be there, I would lay a line of brick dust across each threshold. If someone scoffed at its efficacy, I invited them to have a seat in my client chair and watch how many people in an hour's time walked up to the door, then turned around and walked away. It did not mean they were bad people or brought ill-will. Only that they were not intended to be there. No one who sat and watched walked away still a non-believer.

When anyone acts shocked at the price of brick dust, I invite them to my house to help make the brick dust. We pull our red clay bricks from a barn here in our town that is over a hundred years old. Once they go through the physi-cal demands of using a masonry drill, sledgehammer, rock hammer, three sets of classifiers, weighing, and packaging the new brick dust, they no longer question why it costs more than ground eggshells.

In the Kate Hudson movie, she has a large trough full of red brick dust and flings it around like it is an endless sup-ply. I will guarantee you that almost no rootworker, Witch, or conjurer has that much brick dust in one place at one time.

To use brick dust, cascarilla, salt, or any other boundary agent, sweep down the threshold well and then sprinkle a line of dust from one doorjamb to the other. If your threshold has a metal plate over it, I recommend unscrewing it, pulling it up, laying the brick dust under the plate, then reattaching the plate over the brick dust. It will work exactly the same and will not get easily swept or washed away.

Foot Track Work

One of the most versatile ways to "lay tricks" in Hoodoo is by using a person's footprint or "foot track." If the person makes the footprint while barefoot, all the better. A person's foot track holds tremendous power. It not only contains DNA through direct contact if they are shoeless, but also informs where they are, everywhere they have walked, and everywhere they will go.

A person can work either with the footprint as it lays in the dirt or can collect the footprint dirt to use at a different location.

To keep someone tied to you, find a footprint made when they are walking away from you and drive a rusty square nail into the heel of the print.

To curse a person, carefully collect the dirt containing the imprint of their foot and load it into a jar. Add Goofer Dust (a traditional Hoodoo powder), chili powder, broken glass, rusty nails, wasp or dirt dauber nests, and Crossing Powder or Hot Foot Powder to the jar, urinate in it, then shake it fiercely. Take the jar to a forest as far away from you as you can get it and bury it deep in the earth so it will not be disturbed. Traditionally, the jar is thrown into fast moving water that is flowing away from you, but that is now called littering and can get you fined.

Another way to curse a person using a footprint is to find their footprint and whip it soundly with a belt, horsewhip, rope, or strop, screaming threats and damnation as you do so. Just make sure you have the right person's footprint.

Hoodoo employs a variety of powders, dusts, and dirts that work on a target through their footsteps. To get rid of a person, sprinkle Goofer Dust where you know they will walk, such as across their front step. This works well for neighbors who create discord. Goofer Dust is no joke, and you must release any restrictions you have on exactly *how* the Goofer Dust gets rid of them. They might get a great promotion in another state or they might just disappear in the middle of the night. You just never do know with Goofer Dust, so it should only be used by qualified practitioners.

Hot Foot Powder gets people to move into action. Sprinkle it where they will walk or put a tiny bit in their shoes to get someone motivated.

Silver Dimes

When collecting graveyard dirt—which is used for ancestor veneration, to establish peaceful and protective boundaries, and as an additive to many other recipes—the payment rendered to the person in the grave is nine silver dimes. These must be given to every grave from which dirt is harvested.

Silver dimes tied around the ankle warn the wearer if someone is attempting to lay tricks on them using Goofer

Dust. When in the presence of Goofer Dust, the dime will turn black. From a scientific standpoint, a key component of Goofer Dust is sulfur, which reacts with the silver in the dime.

A silver dime is a powerful addition to a gambling talisman. Put a silver dime into a small red flannel bag along with a lucky hand root and some five-finger grass (cinquefoil).

Sweet Jars/Sweet Pots

Called "sugar jars/pots" or "honey jars/pots," depending on the ingredients you used, a sweet jar is used to "sweeten up" the relationship between two people. This can work to reunite a couple struggling in their relationship, to bring together two people who have never had a relationship, or even to sweeten non-romantic relationships, such as those between a parent and child or an employer and employee.

Representations of each person go into the jar. This can be their written names, photographs, nail or hair clippings, body fluids, or other personal items. The trick is that it must balance and match perfectly. If you use the nail clippings of one person, you must use the nail clippings of the second person. If you use a photo of one person, you must use a photo of the second person.

Once the items are in the jar, douse them with honey or sugar water. The quality of honey is irrelevant. You can also use molasses or maple syrup. Once the lid is sealed, shake the jar like mad to make sure everything inside is covered with thick, sticky, sweet stuff. Set the jar on your altar or working area and cut the end off a taper candle so that you can find the wick at the bottom. Light the end of the candle and let the melting wax pool on the lid so that you can stick the candle to the lid using the hardening wax. Let the candle burn down, then bury the jar by the front door of one of the people in the jar to draw them together. I should note here that the addition of the candle to the sweet jar came after the golden age of Hoodoo and is not an authentic Black Belt practice.

You can use the exact spell, done in the same fashion, with vinegar and/or human urine instead of honey, sugar, or syrup to "sour" a relationship between two people. The difference is that you would dispose of the jar by burying it in a remote location rather than by a front doorstep.

Graveyard Dirt

"Do you actually …?"

"I mean, is it really …?"

Yes, it is. Some claim "graveyard dirt" is a colloquial term or some arcane secret code for the herb mullein, but no, mullein is mullein (and a fine herb it is) and graveyard dirt is exactly what the name implies. In this case, there is truth in advertising.

I collect my graveyard dirt for the entire year at midnight on Samhain (October 31) because the veil between the worlds is thinnest at that time and I must be certain I hear the wishes of the dead clearly to honor their dictates for the year. As any conscientious rootworker will tell you, there is a rapport that builds over time with the spirits of a cemetery. When you enter their world, you do so on their terms to achieve the best results and to preserve the integrity of your interaction.

If you open to the stillness of the cemetery and listen, the spirits will tell you what is and is not welcome behavior. It is less about *could* you take dirt from this grave or that one, but *should* you. When you enter a graveyard for communion and harvesting grave dirt, you must remember that you are a guest in the permanent physical home of these spirits. Whether their essence has passed on to another body or not, the grave marks a resting place for their physical representation on earth for the time marked by the gravestone. As such, we treat it with respect, and if their spirit speaks to us, we honor their wishes. We never collect graveyard dirt without permission from the one who rests there. If they are silent, we move along to another grave.

My local cemetery has graves from the 1800s to the 2000s, and I have gone there for the past fourteen years at the time of this writing. Although I visit it many times a year, Samhain is the only night I ever go to that cemetery after dusk and is the only time I collect dirt. The people buried there are familiar to me in death if not in life, and they make it clear that their hospitality ends at dusk. When I take groups of people there to commune with the dead and explore the historical graves, invariably as soon as the sun starts to dip behind the mountain, a gentle breeze picks up and the guests automatically congregate back at the gate as if in a hive mind. *Time to go.*

On Samhain night, however, I approach the gate with my trowel and my heavy plastic bags and ask for entry. Once inside, the question becomes, "Who wants to play this year?" Orbs come up over the graves of those willing to donate some of their graveyard dirt. These are orbs I see with my physical eyes, like the ones viewed in photography. If I bring someone with me, sometimes they see the orbs and sometimes they do not.

I approach each grave with an orb and ask them the location from where they would like for me to take their dirt. They tell me if I should take from the hands, the feet, or the head. My trowel goes in easily regardless of how much rain we have or have not had that year. I take the dirt until they tell me to stop, then I smooth over the grave so it looks as if I was never there and move on to the next one.

Sometimes, they want to visit, so I linger, listening to their stories and sharing time with them. More often, they are all business. I leave each one silver dimes as payment, shoving them into the area where I took the dirt. I have never once found one of the silver dimes while digging in a later year. Perhaps neighborhood children know to come look for buried change in the graveyard on November 1. Perhaps not. Ravens looking for shiny things? Maybe.

The most valued dirt comes from the grave of a law enforcement official known to be without corruption. Those can be difficult to find, but when you do, the protection factor in the dirt is of the highest you can get. Colonel William Knox was sheriff in our town for a short enough time that he allegedly was not (yet) corrupt. He made me wait six years before giving permission to harvest any of his dirt. Since then, some years he gives his dirt and some years he does not.

I often read Hoodoo primers that encourage the use of dirt from a baby's grave. It is my experience that graveyard dirt gets its energy from the spirit of the person buried there. You would not, for instance, want to take the graveyard dirt of a psychopathic killer if you wanted to use it to create a peaceful environment. I love babies as much as the next person, but they are boring from an energetic perspective. They lived very little life, had few experiences, and no matter how beloved they were by all who beheld them, their energy pattern contributes little to the surrounding grave material. Because they did not communicate in life beyond crying for basic needs and cooing when they were happy, I find their communication after death is also minimal. In most cases, I only feel a faint imprint on the baby graves and tend to leave them alone. If I feel anything connected to a baby grave, it is often the grief of the parents. When I feel that, a minor degree of investigating invariably shows that the grave of the parents is adjacent and what I felt was their bleed-over energy.

Graveyard dirt, in addition to serving as a primary ingredient for many Hoodoo recipes, creates the conditions of the grave. When you are dead and buried, there is little anyone can do to harm you, so it acts as a protective ward, especially law enforcement graveyard dirt. It promotes peace, facilitates endings, and encourages releasing what no longer serves us. When in conflict, the user can sprinkle a line of it around the perimeter of a room or a work cubicle, around property boundaries, across a threshold, or even around a bed to minimize negative interaction and bring about a peaceful resolution.

Mojo Bags/Gris Gris

Called a "medicine bag" by the Native Americans and a Gris Gris by New Orleans Hoodoo folks, the mojo bag is more than just a small bag of significant items. It is engaged as a living being that is there to serve the user, sort of like a pet that gets things done. I like to tell people to imagine how a beam of sunlight can start a fire if it shines just right through a drop of water. Your own power is the sunlight, but the mojo is your drop of water. Traditionally a small bag of red or brown flannel or cotton, the mojo should always have an odd number of items in it to keep the energy off balance. If the energy in it balances, the mojo will go dormant.

When I make one, it starts with a stone that lends the energy I want to create. I think of the stone as the beating heart of the mojo. I then add herbs sympathetic to the cause. Each herb counts as its own item. Next, I add a piece of natural cotton liberally doused with an empowered oil that supports the goal. I then tie up the bag with a ribbon of the correct color and either clip a charm onto the ribbon or put it inside the bag.

I put all the mojos to sleep until someone needs one, then I wake it up through breath and massage and bind it to them using the same oils as are on the cotton inside, and an anointing process. The user may add to the mojo as they feel inclined to do so, but must add items two at a time to keep the odd number going. The mojo bag stays with them always, worn in a bra, carried in a pocket or purse, put inside their pillowcase at night, or resting on a nightstand or altar. They feed their mojo tiny bits of supportive oil two or three times a week.

Crossroads Magic

Like many other spiritual paths, the crossroads is sacred in Hoodoo practice. In Voodoo, Papa Legba often appears at the crossroads, representative of the spiritual crossroads he guards.

A crossroads is anyplace where two roads intersect. It is a powerful place because when you are at a crossroads, you are everywhere and nowhere at the same time.

There are two different types of crossroads, each of which you can easily visualize. The first is the most common crossroads, which is when two roads cross over one another. This is called a female crossroads. The second is a fork in the road where one road divides into two roads, each leading off into a separate direction. This is a male crossroads. Certain traditional spells call for the dirt of a "three-way" or a "male" crossroads and others may call for a "four-way" or "four corners" or "female" crossroads. Most spells do not specify, and in that case, the dirt from either may be used.

Leaving an offering of twenty-one pennies and lighting three red candles at a crossroads and waiting as they burn down is said to remove all blockages and obstacles from your path.

Because the veil between the worlds is naturally thin at the crossroads, go there if you need to speak to your ancestors for advice.

The crossroads will receive and dispose of used magical items once a spell is completed. (If your spellwork is particularly aggressive, tradition dictates you must bury the leavings in a cemetery).

If you wish to master any talent, bring the tools of your intended trade to the crossroads and practice after dark for nine nights straight. Bring a candle with you and remain at the crossroads each night until the candle burns down. You must not show fear to any animal or person who meets you there during the time of your practice. Anyone or anything that comes is part of your learning process.

If you have no crossroads nearby where you can safely work, many practitioners sell crossroads dirt, carefully collected from the four corners and center of a crossroads. The crossroads dirt I sell comes from the intersection of a road used by the Pony Express in the 1800s. Using crossroads dirt, you can trace out a plus sign on the ground or even on your floor and effectively create your own crossroads anywhere. If you collect and use crossroads dirt, be sure to identify the gender aspect of the crossroads when you store it.

Crossroads dirt is also great for decision-making. If you cannot see the best choice to make, lay out your crossroads dirt in an equalateral cross and sit where the lines intersect with one of the arms of the crossroads to your back.

Say "The past is behind me. To my left, my right, and before me, all possibilities lie. Show me what I am to do." Sit in the crossroads until your spirit tells you it is time to get up. While you are there, clear your mind and go into a meditative state. If insight comes to you, file it away for future consideration. If not, pay close attention to signs and omens over the next few days. The answer will come to you.

PART 2

APPALACHIAN
GRANNY MAGIC

—— 8 ——
About Granny Magic

By far the most reclusive and unexplored of our three primary folk magic paths, the magic of the Appalachian and Ozark Mountains is a significant beat in the pulse of the history of the eastern United States. Granny Magic, also called "Mountain Magic," is also the tradition of the three that is fading away into history the fastest. It is dear to me because it speaks to the magic of my childhood growing up in rural Kentucky.

One must dig deep to find information on these practices, not only because much of the tradition was transferred by oral rather than written means, but also because each community was isolated and developed its own set of practices and beliefs based on a blended Scotch-Irish history. Like the immigrants who settled in the eastern American mountains, the traditions they brought with them dug in and evolved, each in its own fashion. Eventually, individual villages did the same types of folk magic work with their own unique twists that grew and changed through the generations. Working from memory and experience alone, since many of the teachings were never recorded, the Scotch-Irish healing wisdom became a game of "telephone" through the ages, with the message changed a bit by each interpretation.

The continuation of a common ancestral practice within extremely remote areas created separate bubbles of variations on the same theme. It is said that the Scotch-Irish magical traditions were preserved with greater persistence and accuracy in these areas than they were in Scotland or Ireland, due to the isolation of mountain communities from outside influence. Rarely did people from one village even venture to visit other nearby villages, not only because of the difficulty in travel, but also due to their clan-based culture that was singularly focused on the well-being of the people in the immediate area.

Even the pronunciation of words is hotly debated. Where I grew up in rural Kentucky, "Appalachia" was pronounced "App-uh-LAY-sha" and I never heard anyone there say it differently. In South Carolina, however, the pronunciation is "App-uh-LATCH-uh," and anyone who says it otherwise is considered uneducated and clearly an outsider. From what I can ascertain, the variance lies in whether one is in northern Appalachia or the southern regions.

When I first presented information on the origins of Granny Magic a few years before this writing, I was informed that "no self-respecting Scot in their right mind would ever identify as 'Scotch-Irish.'" Another person told me, "People are Scots, 'scotch' is whiskey." Aside from the fact that scotch is just called whisky (without the e) in Scotland, the prevailing academia shows that the descendants of the original immigrants who settled this area still refer to themselves and their ancestors as "Scotch-Irish," and that throughout history the label of "Scotch-Irish" is the preferred terminology used over "Scot-Irish."

With profound and righteous indignation, the people from each mountain area defend their dialect, and by extension, their healing and conjuring practices. The isolation that preserved their traditions so well also created a sense of aloneness in the world, which can make the incorporation of new ideas and other perspectives a challenge. It is difficult to adequately explain how small a village is when compared to the rest of the world, but how large it is when it is your only world.

9

Types of Practitioners

Appalachian and Ozark Granny Magic included special-ized practices usually taught early in life. Within Granny Magic, there are four primary types of practitioners: granny doctors, goomer doctors, seers, and water witches. The only times mountain people use the word "witch" with respect or acceptance is when they refer to dowsing for water. Otherwise, a strong regional stigma insisted that witches were evil people in league with the devil, fixed on ruining the life of good, God-fearing Christians.

None of these four types of workers possessed powers themselves. Their abilities were bestowed upon them through the grace of God and they acted as channels for God's power. Much like the root, the herb, the branch, or any other item used in folk medicine, healers in the Scotch-Irish traditions considered themselves natural tools to enact God's will on earth. None of these practices were gender-specific, although one gender often dominated the field due to convenience of circumstances rather than any imposed societal restrictions.

Often working in unity, these practitioners exerted their influence in mundane matters of the community, such as crop planning, planting, and harvesting, as well as animal care and healing of both people and animals. They worked the weather, gave advice, and provided support to those within the village.

A person who apprenticed with an experienced healer was usually one who showed proclivity toward a certain talent or inherited it through family lines. Healers chose their apprentices based on considerations such as an expressed passion for or interest in a practice at a young age, the endorsement of a seer who saw that it was the person's path to apprentice to a vocation, or because the elder sensed that a descendant was the appropriate successor to take up the mantle. There were usually multiple practitioners in any of the four fields, due to necessity as much as tradition.

Granny Women, Healers, Yarb Doctors, and Root Doctors

Although Granny Magic is a term *we* now use to describe the folk magic born in the Appalachian and Ozark areas, the actual people who developed and practiced it did not. They considered what they did to be divine, not magical.

They did, however, use the word "Granny" to describe the granny women who were healers and midwives. "Yarb doctor" (derived from "herb doctor") and "root doctor" (adopting the Hoodoo nomenclature) were also interchangeable titles identifying the same type of practitioner: someone who heals the body by way of folk medicine, using God-given ingredients such as herbs, roots, flowers, and other natural resources.

Although some men acted as healers, women dominated the field, as is reflected by the titles of "granny doctor" or "granny women." A male was a yarb doctor or a root doctor and was addressed with the title of "Doctor" followed by the surname, such as "Doctor Hardin" as we do today, or "Doc Hardin" in the familiar. A woman could also be a yarb doctor or root doctor, but most often, the "granny" delineation was reserved for female healers, followed by the healer's surname, such as "Granny Jenkins." An illness or injury might have someone saying "Best go get Dr. Davis," or "Go find Granny Stillwater."

Females dominated the field because of the connection of healing to midwifery and child care. With no physicians in these mountain villages, the ability of the granny women to effectively manage illness and injury was paramount to the survival of individuals and the village itself. The blended cultures of the Native American, the Scotch-Irish, and the Hoodoo rootworkers allowed the healing practices of all three cultures to grow and increase in effectiveness. By working together, all three traditions evolved and thrived.

Granny women, yarb doctors, and root doctors made poultices, concoctions, decoctions, tinctures, salves, and a full pharmacopeia of natural treatments. Their primary scope of treatment was the physical body with its full range of potential injuries and ailments, as well as natural conditions such as childbirth and menopausal symptoms.

One granny doctor with whom most Americans, particularly those of the Baby Boomer age, are familiar, is Daisy Moses, who is more commonly remembered as Granny Clampett on the Filmways television show *The Beverly Hillbillies*. Although portrayed by the show's writers and actor Irene Ryan as a campy caricature of a granny doctor, "Doctor Granny," as she was called, is not that far off from the historical reality. Her use of moonshine, tinctures, potions, and "hillbilly" superstition is only a mildly exaggerated version of what a typical granny doctor might have been in the 1700–1800s. Of course, all parody carries within it some level of truth, and this example is not too far off the mark.

Granny Clampett frequently expounded on the virtues of her "spring tonic." It was commonly believed that the rigors of winter took its toll on the body and weakened the system, so when spring finally came, a tonic was necessary to bring the body back to life once more.

When someone took to their sickbed and worsened or when a baby was coming, Granny would drop everything and tend to those who needed her care. If the condition was not too serious, the patient might go to the healer themselves, knowing she had shelves of tonics, herbs, roots, and other cures to manage any health crisis that developed.

Goomer Doctors, Conjure Doctors, and Power Doctors

Unlike the granny doctors with their use of natural substances for physical healing, goomer doctors, conjure doctors, and power doctors worked in chants, charms, spells, amulets, breath, touch, and incantations. The titles shifted through regional variances, but all identified the same kind of healer. Using the power of psalms or other scriptures, their job was to cure maladies of all kinds through what we would identify as "straight out magic," although they would never themselves define it as such.

Stopping the flow of blood, curing warts, or drawing the fire out of a burn or fever ("drawin' out the farr") were all within the purview of the goomer doctor, healing with their charms, chants, scripture recitation, and incantations alongside the granny woman with her poultices and tinctures. In addition to scripture and other chanted treatments, tools of the power doctors included charms, amulets, exorcisms, conjures, jacks, and jujus, all of which relied fully upon the power of faith within the victim and the family of the victim.

Goomer is a word that means "bewitch," and one of a goomer doctor's primary functions was to reverse curses, hexes, and witchcraft worked against a person who was symptomatic of a crossing. Sometimes these workers were called "witch masters" or "witch doctors" and their repertoire included spells to kill suspected witches.

Power doctors worked primarily from a protective and defensive position. If a person felt they were crossed by someone else, they sought out the power doctor, conjure doctor, or goomer doctor to "uncross" them through incantations and charms.

As much as the power doctors worked to keep their clients safe, there is plenty of evidence to demonstrate that they were not averse to a proactive and offensive approach. In its edition published on June 19, 1939, *Life* magazine ran a photo of an elderly woman working with a wax poppet, with the caption, "Ozark 'witch-woman' makes a doll of dirt and beeswax, names it after her enemy. She drives nails into the doll's body to 'hurt' corresponding parts of enemy's body."

In the same issue of *Life*, historian Vance Randolph published photographs depicting a reproduction of a "witch altar" he allegedly saw "done by a girl who was witchin' the girl who stole her man. A real human skull was placed on top of a Bible, and before it were placed two dolls—one to represent her husband and the other to represent the girl. The poppet used to represent the girl had four big nails driven into it's [sic] back."

In an extensive set of memoirs and letters called the "Paul Eliot Green Papers," the author quotes a magical work from a power doctor in Tennessee who instructs, "Wet a rag in the blood of your enemy and put it behind a rock in the chimney. When it rots, your enemy will die."

Goomer doctors taught their craft generationally, as did the granny doctors; however, goomer doctors taught only relatives of the opposite gender. This practice meant that there were more male goomer doctors than yarb doctors, since the need for a male student occurred every other generation. This tradition of teaching the opposite gender, which appears universal across most of the isolated communities, traces back to the Irish cunning-folk of Ulster and into the Scottish clan practices.

Other conditions that are not so consistent include the belief that a charm can be taught to each person only once or its power will drain away. Another says that a teacher may instruct an apprentice no more than three times for each charm, and after that the individual may no longer use the charm, as it is clearly not intended for them.

Many popular nursery rhymes come from the chants goomer doctors used to manipulate the weather or to ward off evil. A favorite is "Rain, rain, go away. Come again another day," which is an English weather charm that followed into Appalachian practice.

Neither granny doctors nor the goomer doctors charged their patients for the care they provided. Patients and their families might offer gifts or services in exchange to show their appreciation, but payment was not required. Healing the people in these communities was expected of those blessed by God with the ability to do so. In deference to their natural or learned talents, villagers held both goomer doctors and granny doctors in great esteem as holy people, much as the witch doctor and the shaman in other traditions garnered respect as holy leaders.

Many talented healers performed the duties of both goomer doctor and granny doctor, treating with herbs and magical charms at the same time, much like the two-headed doctor in Hoodoo.

Seers

Although their skills proved useful in diagnosis, seers were not specifically healers, but more of prognosticators who read omens and signs provided by natural occurrences. They sought guidance from oracles and through divination to influence and inform decisions made by individuals or by the community.

The role of seers fell primarily to women, passed on from mother to daughter with "the sight," "second sight," "the knowing," or "the gift." They read tea leaves and animal entrails; watched the migration and other behavior of animals; observed the stars, clouds, and other astronomical or meteorological events; and monitored what we would call "superstitions," such as a broom falling to the floor or the itching of a body part with no apparent cause.

Interpreting the dreams of others and relating their own prophetic dreams provided insight into what a seer perceived as wisdom or messages from God. In cases of dire need, a seer would take a mild narcotic to induce lucid dreaming and bring on visions.

The seers scryed not only in bowls of water but also in dirt, by reading the patterns created in the loose soil by air movement. Seers would use a stick to etch out a rough circle in the loose dirt, then call in the winds and watch as the air moved the dirt into readable forms which the seer would then interpret.

Flame and coal scrying for visioning was yet another way God spoke to these revelators. Although mirrors are used for scrying now, in the 1700s and 1800s, they were quite expensive and few homes owned them. The same is true for specialty scrying items such as crystal balls, so ordinary items took the place of these now traditional tools.

Water Witches and Witch Wigglers

Although water witching implies dowsing for water, in actual practice, these talented and vital community members dowsed for many purposes other than deciding where to sink a well. Their specialized techniques enabled them to find specific metals in the earth or locate missing objects. I remember my grandfather "water witching" to find where to dig for coal in his mine. "Witch wigglers" refers to the "wiggle" at the end of the stick(s) when water is close by.

Appalachian and Ozark people took the art of dowsing quite seriously and used water witches when digging a well, building a house, laying their garden, finding lost items, or even positioning a grave, to locate the ideal placement.

Water witching is the only Appalachian folk magic practice dominated by males, but as with the other gender role assignments of this area, women were not forbidden from practicing water witchery. The practice fell quite naturally to men since they were the ones sinking the wells, digging the graves, and laying in the gardens.

Dowsing rods follow the ley lines of energy running unseen along the earth's surface, and in this fashion, could also locate holy areas and sacred spaces. The closer that the target of the dowsing, such as water, energy, or metal, lay to the surface of the earth, the stronger the pull on the dowsing rod and the faster the dowser could read the results.

Although some historians insist a dowsing rod is a straight stick and not forked as so often shown, nearly all authentic photos I located in exhaustive research for this book showed a forked stick either turned inward or outward from the dowser. Most agree that the dowsing rod could be up to three feet long and came from the wood of a flowering tree such as dogwood, apple, or peach.

My grandfather owned two types of dowsing apparatuses. The first was a traditional forked rod made from dogwood. The second was a set of two hand-forged, thin metal rods, each in an L shape, that looked like large, skinny allen wrenches. He held the smaller end of one of the metal L shapes in each hand with the longer ends extending outward, resting between his thumbs and forefingers. As he got closer to the target, the longer ends would start to sway back and forth until they eventually met in the middle.

The wooden dowsing rod he used with a branch of each of the forked ends lightly held between his thumb and forefinger. He would pace the area he surveyed with the dowsing rod, and eventually the single end of the rod would turn downward, which told him where to dig. My grandfather, "Pa

Mitchell," died when I was five years old, so these memories come from a very young and long-ago perspective.

Water witchers also used simple pendulums of metal, sometimes a fishing weight or a stone tied to the end of a natural string. The weight would swing back and forth and follow either the ley line or the path of the flowing groundwater below.

— 10 —
The History
and Development
of Granny Magic

The history of Granny Magic began early on, as the Christian Church established dominance in Britain over many hundreds of years, squelching out the nature-based religions and forbidding the veneration of the old gods. The first to adopt the new religion were the royal and noble classes, who considered Christianity to be a more enlightened and elite spirituality. Because the wealthier classes came first to the new religion, magical practices from earlier times prevailed longer in less affluent areas, even as they embraced the new Christianized theologies.

While the ancient spiritual ways fell out of favor among the wealthy, the use of charms, rhymes, spells, and healing by touch remained an ongoing practice for those of lower social status. Commoners without physicians used practical folk healing with impunity, for it was rarely associated with Witchcraft, the bane of both the Catholic and Protestant Churches.

Over time, the poorer people of Europe established a comfortable blend of Christian beliefs and ancestral healing practices. From their perspective, religion itself was a supernatural experience, so magical concepts governing healing, controlling weather, and ensuring a fine harvest integrated seamlessly with the biblical and religious processes and influences.

In the 1600s, the king of Scotland, England, and Ireland was James I (or James VI if you were in Scotland, although they were the same man). A major ambition of King James was to find a way to eliminate the ongoing conflict with the Scots who lived close to the border between England and Scotland. When Scotland and England were separate countries frequently at war, the unruly and unmanageable Scots in the lowlands were an asset for border control. Now that he was king of both countries, the rowdy border Scots who favored clan over crown were difficult to control and contentious to the new king's rule. A primary problem in the lands along the border of Scotland and England was that of too many people and not enough land.

Ireland was also a thorn in his side, persisting in rampant Catholicism well beyond the conversion of England to Protestantism. An advisor to King James named Hugh Montgomery, who was himself a Scottish lord tormented by the aggressive lowland Scots, suggested that the monarch could solve two problems at once by offering the troublesome borderers a half million or so acres of land in Ulster, a turmoil-ridden territory in Northern Ireland.

By offering free land in Ulster, the king hoped to relocate thousands of the antagonistic Scots to Ireland, far enough away from British borders so as not to be a problem, and at the same time instigate a huge injection of Protestant subjects into the predominantly Catholic Ireland. From there, he theorized, nature and attrition would take over and the fecund and aggressive Scots would quickly spread Protestantism throughout Ireland, eventually pushing out Catholicism as the dominant religion.

As predicted, thousands of Scottish farmers, preachers, prisoners, and other people of the lowlands, as well as some British people, took the king up on his offer and immigrated to Northern Ireland, establishing communities and farms there. Over the next hundred years, the Scottish and Irish blended their cultures and intermittently battled with one other and with the British Crown. Both the Scots and the Irish were warriors at heart, and their eagerness to protect their land and their families generated frequent conflicts, as did growing persecution from the English.

Throughout the 1700s, political and religious persecution persisted and, in fact, intensified in Ulster. Penal laws imposed by the English treated the Scotch-Irish, who were Presbyterians, as second-class citizens, subservient to the elite Episcopalians. Presbyterian marriages were declared invalid, known Presbyterians could no longer hold public office, and even their ministers were defrocked.

After a century of farming inhospitable soil, suffering through a drought of many years, and enduring unbearable political strife, over 200,000 people ultimately migrated from Ulster into the Appalachians and Ozarks of America in the 1700s. The 1800s saw an influx of another million or so Scotch-Irish immigrating to this area.

America was the number one exporter of flax seed, a primary commodity in Europe. Ship captains who brought tons of flax seed into Scotland and Northern England would normally return across the Atlantic with an empty hull, but they quickly found that their embellished stories of life in America provided them with ample human cargo for their journey back to the New World. This provided them a substantial income for crossing the ocean in both directions rather than only one.

Enticed by the promise of abundant land and freedoms unavailable to them in Ireland, the Scotch-Irish poured into the ships returning to America, often unaware that they would spend up to three months packed into the ship's hold without hygiene or privacy, and often lacking sufficient food or water.

Whole families traveled together, bringing only what they could carry in small bags. They would make furniture, clothing, or other necessities that they needed when they arrived and settled. What they did have was a devout personal relationship with God, a love of music and liquor, and years of ancestral experience in healing, working the land, and animal husbandry.

The Scotch-Irish who immigrated to the United States in the 1700–1800s settled into the harshest regions of the Appalachian and Ozark mountains, bringing with them a rich magical system developed from the blending of Scottish and Irish folk healing practices of the common people. These hearty, stalwart settlers left a terrain even more brutal than the one they found and settled within pockets of untamed mountain country throughout Kentucky, Tennessee, Virginia, Maryland, West Virginia, and North Carolina; as far south as northern Alabama, Georgia, and western South Carolina; and as far north as Pennsylvania, southern Ohio, and parts of southern upstate New York.

The Appalachian Mountains span 205,000 miles from southern New York to northern Mississippi. Geological and archeological evidence indicates that Cherokee settled this area in approximately 500 CE. The region was painfully inhospitable, and immigrants from other countries favored the rich and more accommodating lands further west. The Scotch-Irish, however, were accustomed to living in harsh environments and the difficult life settling there presented did not put them off at all.

Over the next hundred years, they established strong clan-based communities in the remote and mountainous regions of the eastern and southeastern American colonies. Rather than suffering from the isolation of the deep mountains, these hearty people embraced the opportunity to live in freedom, out from under the oppression of the British Crown and without the dictates of other paradigms ruling over them. Here, they could create their own rules, choose their own morality, and establish their own culture. That is exactly what they did.

Those settling in the Appalachian area were Church of England dissenters, Presbyterians, and Calvinists. Some moved on into the Ozark Mountains of Arkansas, Missouri, and Oklahoma, where they integrated with the German Lutherans and Anabaptists who brought the influence of Pennsylvania Dutch Pow-wow magic into their practices and beliefs.

The local Native American tribes did not practice individual property ownership and believed that the land belonged to everyone. The Scotch-Irish, however, were territorial, and their subsequent establishment of farming areas and homesteads interrupted the hunting and traveling movement of the Native Americans, sometimes resulting in fierce conflict. Over time, the two cultures established an uneasy tolerance, which eventually led to a cooperative working relationship.

Native American tribes of the Appalachian and Ozark Mountains, primarily the Cherokee, Creek, and Shawnee, traded their knowledge of healing and other folk magic techniques with the settlers. Likewise, the African American migration north during the post-Reconstruction era brought the Hoodoo influence into Appalachian and Ozark magical practice during the late 1800s.

This melting pot of cultural factors in small, remote communities created a pattern of rich, vibrant practices of healing and crisis management, all based on the Scotch-Irish framework with Hoodoo and Native American influences. Although their origins were the same, the subsequent development was quite individual due to the isolation of communities from one another and from the outside world. The result was that each clan or community independently created their own system of healing and Bible study based on their memories of common ancestral beliefs.

Native Americans taught the settlers about the flora and fauna in the mountainous areas, including what roots, herbs, barks, and other natural plant matter they could substitute for the materials used in Ireland for the same purposes. The Scotch-Irish taught the Native Americans about the use of charms, scriptures, and the power of breath in healing.

Intermarriage and tribal adoption between the two cultures became common. The Native American tribes were matrilineal—meaning that lineage flowed from mother to child—rather than embracing the patriarchal position of the Roman-influenced Europeans. Although England was a fiercely patriarchal country in the 1700–1800s, many of the Scottish and Irish clans still held onto their pre-Roman ancestral beliefs of a matrilineal family line, which made for a more affable assimilation with Native American traditions.

This comfort with matriarchal power created a strong gender equality within the Appalachian and Ozark communities, affording women an equal and sometimes dominant position in healing and magical work, as well as within the home, through fosterage of respect for the female influence. This perspective was likely a strong component in the gender-neutral approach to healing roles in the mountain communities.

Called "cunning-folk" in Europe, mountain folk healers held a long-standing tradition of Conjure, faith-based, and herbal healing practices. The unchallenged acceptance of lay healers that was common to Ireland in the 1600s continued in the clan-based communities of the Colonies. In this culture, men typically worked in the fields or hunted to supplement the larders, leaving the practices of healing and child care to women. Men were not discouraged from practicing the healing arts if they were called to do so by God or showed a proclivity toward it. Women also worked in the fields and cared for livestock alongside the men. Everyone pitched in to do what needed to be done for the safety, nourishment, and perpetuity of the clan, without the complexity of gender biases.

It was a reasonable extension of the concept of women as the givers of life to also consider women the sustainers of life. Granny Magic grew out of midwifery, which was a female-dominated practice. Experienced mothers naturally congregated around loved ones as they labored in childbirth, to offer support and share the benefit of their own experiences. After attending many such births, the ability to manage complications in childbirth, as well as prenatal problems, created a culture of lay midwifery.

This branched off into care for newborns, children, and eventually most health-related issues within the individual communities. Granny doctors were so called because the most revered and experienced healers were often older women, sometimes with a younger apprentice. "Granny" was a title of honor bestowed by the community upon those oldest and most experienced healers.

Isolated as they were from the mainstream of American society or any form of urban structure, autonomy and self-sufficiency were crucial to the Appalachian and Ozark people. Throughout the 1700s and most of the 1800s, there were no churches, doctors, stores, or schools in Appalachian and Ozark communities. Therefore, it was essential that healers know how to manage all forms of illness and injury, as well as natural conditions such as childbirth and menopause. Roads did not exist until the 1930s, so access even by wagon or horse could prove challenging. Even now, many roads remain unpaved.

Granny Magic itself had a primary focus on healing, but its scope also involved romance, protection, and relationships of the home and family. Prosperity magic did not typically focus on the individual, but on the harvest and the sustainability of the community. Personal magic looked more toward harmonious family and community relations. Generalized "good fortune" and living a "good life," rather than financial abundance, were emphasized. What we think of as spellwork in Granny Magic used the simplest of tools and required no great preparation. Much of it happened on the fly and the only intensive study involved learning from your elders unless one received a calling into an apprenticeship.

Granny Magic was and remains a generational practice, usually passed from parent to child or grandparent to grandchild. Rarely did anyone teach a person outside of their family or clan structure, and often one family constituted the "healers" in a village, although a village could have multiple healers as well as different types of healers. Geographical and temporal variances accounted for differences in practices that might appear contradictory but usually achieved similar results and, when analyzed, were frequently variations of the same theme of treatment.

An example in modern parlance is that one parent might reduce a child's fever with a tepid bath and plenty of fluids, while another parent might use an over-the-counter fever medication and bed rest. Although not the same approach, both treatments would probably bring satisfactory results. Likewise, a granny doctor in one village might treat a fever with white willow bark and another with an apple cider vinegar foot bath.

Within these mountain communities in the 1600–1800s, most of the people were illiterate, so healing and magical traditions transferred by way of verbal communication rather than through text or other written instruction. This factor alone resulted in the loss of a tremendous amount of folk wisdom transferred in healer apprenticeships, as information was forgotten, misunderstood, altered, or amended. It did, however, create a growing, ever-evolving legacy of practices with some historical modalities retained throughout.

Most Scotch-Irish families in Appalachia lived in a multi-generational homestead and experienced abject poverty beyond what most Americans today can imagine.

Music was an important societal component, and the Scotch-Irish are credited for bringing the fiddle to America, which is why the instrument figures so prominently in bluegrass music. They kept alive traditional songs from Scotland and Ireland through community dances and gatherings. Music, ancestral rhyming through nursery rhymes and jingles, and dancing, specifically clogging, held special places in their recreational and spiritual lives.

In each area, communities worked in intimate concert with the spirit of their immediate environment, and a person had to know their own land and its unique idiosyncrasies to survive. Like their European ancestors, Appalachian and Ozark people knew that their very survival was tied to the land through agriculture, the hunting of wild animals, and animal husbandry, so it makes sense that they wove those vital factors into their spirituality. They needed to study and understand the behavior of wildlife, wind, rain, and sun, and fully grasp the nature of, well, *nature* in their specific community in order to thrive. They could not rule over it. So, to survive they had to become a part of it and work in concert with its local nuances.

Churches did not appear in the area until the Great Revival, also called the Great Awakenings, of the 1800s, which brought lay ministers into the mountains with their portable camp meetings. This resulted in mass conversions from Presbyterian to Baptist and Methodist faiths and introduced the concepts of public repentance and being "saved" through the intervention of Christ and the minister. Suddenly, mountain people who remained isolated their entire lives would travel many miles to attend a "camp meeting." One such gathering in Virginia in 1801 boasted more than twenty-five thousand attendees from the mountain regions.

Prior to this, spiritual guidance in these communities came in the form of prayer meetings and Bible studies conducted informally in village homes, led either by the person in the village who could read or the village elders or both. Often, they quoted scripture from memory rather than reading it, and they were Bible literalists without room for religious allegory, metaphors, or variations in translation. They treated each scripture as absolute and not open to individual interpretation.

What we now identify as folk magic—defined as the practical application of supernatural practices by common people to a cultural lifestyle—was not an isolated activity separate from their day-to-day experience. It came naturally to them and was heavily integrated into the fabric of their communities and home lives. They tossed salt over their shoulders after accidentally spilling it with the same mindset that a modern person has when turning on the car's headlights at dusk. It was second nature and made perfect sense. No one had to convince anyone else that the magic worked. It simply did, and they accepted this as their reality without question.

— 11 —
Basic Beliefs of Granny Magic

Granny Magic flourished as these communities developed within the deepest regions of the Ozark and the Appalachian Mountains. The mindset of anyone who settled and lived in this area was one of externalization, and their natural proclivity was to help others. Concepts of "southern hospitality" derive to some degree from this propensity for reaching out to help those around you. In conditions as untenable as the rocky and cold land of Ulster and the isolated, harsh mountainous areas of the United States, no person could be an island and hope to survive, much less thrive. They might be suspicious of outsiders, but if a crisis arose, they would help.

An interwoven network of support was vital to the continuity of each village, and every person within the community was essential to the success of that village. This premise was as instrumental to the birth of Granny Magic as the matrilineal clan precepts and ancestral influences.

The Foundations of Mountain Spirituality

We could accurately sum up the overall belief system as "nature-based Christian spirituality." The hill folk believed that God reveals himself to us in two very distinct ways: through nature and through scripture. Granny Magic healers combined both into their practices as necessary and complementary components.

Through the expressions of God in nature, God approaches humans. For instance, jewelweed is a natural treatment for the effects of poison ivy and it frequently grows in the near proximity of poison ivy. To a person living in these mountain communities in 1700–1900, this was evidence of God's divine plan and how God takes care of us. The common belief was, "God did not create any illness without also creating the cure. It is up to us to find it."

Although the beliefs described here might seem overly rigid and dogmatic, there is evidence of flexibility and evolving practice within the history of Granny Magic. Modern inventions such as trains, automobiles, and umbrellas sparked the development of new superstitions and traditions, such as never opening an umbrella in the house or the use of train tracks in magical work. It is through these integrations of innovation that we see Mountain Magic as an adaptive culture inclusive of new components that complimented their already flourishing traditions.

Mountain people did not believe in animism. Rocks were rocks, herbs were herbs, and roots were roots, without soul, spirit, or inherent energy assigned to them. God reached out to humans through the plant, the rock, or the root, and it was the spirit of God, not that of the plant, rock, or root, that healed. Likewise, it was not the person who healed, but God healing through the person.

There was no pantheism, except in the form of the Holy Trinity of God the Father, Jesus the Son, and the Holy Spirit. God the Father was the God of all things, a largely unapproachable divinity that was the creative force, an overlord who commanded every experience and held the patterns of fate for each human life. God sat in judgment of us all and ultimately decided if we were worthy to enter Heaven based on how we led our lives. On Judgment Day, goats—the unworthy—went to the left, and sheep—the worthy—assembled on his right side.

Jesus the Son was the intercessor, as the Bible says in John 14:6: *"I am the way and the truth and the life. No one comes to the Father except through me."* As the personal savior, Jesus was approachable where God was not. Jesus came to earth at the behest of God the Father to live a human life and then to sacrifice that human life in atonement for original sin. This gave Jesus the distinction of being a liaison between humans and God, becoming a gateway that assured a heavenly afterlife through his sacrifice and subsequent resurrection. One only gained redemption and salvation through the intercession of Jesus, and more importantly, his favor.

The Holy Spirit was the divine essence of God made manifest in the physical realm to provide comfort, protection, and healing. Also called the Holy Ghost, it was the center of and bringer of life, connected to all people through the soul level. Nature was a direct manifestation of the Holy Spirit and provided signs, omens, and portents to guide humans in the unveiling and enactment of God's plan. Goomer doctors summoned the Holy Spirit through breath, charms, and psalms to heal, to assist in the understanding of scripture, or to comfort in times of need.

Spirituality in the mountains included the concept of fatalism, meaning that while we are humans doing human things, ultimately, all experiences in a lifetime were the will of God, pre-determined at birth and immutable. Achieving the goal of leading a good life meant understanding one's place in God's divine plan and in the overall will of God, enduring the strife God intended for us with grace, and enjoying the blessings he sent to us with humility. As surely as God granted his blessings, he could take them away to punish an untoward display of pride.

The livelihood and security of everyone in the community depended strongly on a good harvest, healthy animals, an accurate weather forecast, and large families to provide plenty of hands to perform the many tasks required for survival. The level of work ethic was impressive, with children learning very early on to plant, sew, weave, hunt, and invest in the important work that sustained the village.

The folk magic practices of this area focused on practical needs such as weather control and prediction, agriculture management, healing of animals and people, animal husbandry, and fertility of all kinds. The folk healers of the area addressed all of those concerns between them.

Crops, Animal Husbandry & the Weather

Granny women and seers dictated the time of planting and harvesting of crops, as well as when to hunt, when to fish, and when to cull the herds of livestock. Careful attention went to the moon sign and phase, which they referenced differently than our current astrological layout does. Instead of referring to signs in which to plant, the classic zodiac images became parts of the body.

Corn, for instance, is best planted in the sign of the breast (Cancer) or the arms (Gemini), but corn must not go to ground until the elm leaves are the size of a squirrel's ear, oak leaves are the size of a mouse's ear, and the apple blossoms are falling. Flowers blossom best when planted in the kidneys (Libra). If you plant beans in the arms, they will bloom well, but not bear fruit.

One should only plant above-ground crops between the new moon and the full, but not until the daffodils bloom and the lilac leaves are fully budded. When the lilac blooms fade for the year, it is time to plant cucumbers and squash. The first killing frost will always come three months after you hear the first katydid sing.

Everything from butchering animals and getting a haircut to pulling teeth and canning vegetables had an associated astrological influence, and the traditions often contradicted one another from region to region.

Historian Vance Randolph, in his book *Ozark Magic and Folklore*, talks about a Christian group that "held public prayers for 'that feller in Springfield that lies so much about the weather.'" He was referencing the mountain peoples' disdain for a man named C. C. Williford, one of the first weather reporters in the nation. Williford delivered weather reports on radio station KWTO in Springfield, Missouri, every morning except Sunday. Appalachian people were slow to accept or trust the new science of weather forecasting, and instead held doggedly to their observances of the signs of nature to tell when and how the weather would change.

Nature provided many omens to foretell the coming weather, often in sufficient time that the local folk magic practitioners could shift it to a more favorable outcome.

Granny Witch Byron Ballard identifies a sign as a "natural, observed occurrence such as nature providing indications of when to plant crops." An omen, however, is a "natural and observed occurrence that is *unusual*, such as unusual behavior in plants or animals" (Ballard 2012, 55). The waxing moon is a natural, observed occurrence that happens on the regular and is a sign to plant crops that grow underground. Birds flying in a strange pattern may be natural and observed but is also *unusual*, so a seer might interpret that as an omen.

Certain natural processes, such as leaves exposing their undersides, could predict rain, as could a halo around the moon. Two woodpeckers sharing a tree or thick husks growing on corn indicated a cold, harsh winter. A cat washing over its ear promised fair weather.

Marriage and Weddings

Girls married early, usually between the ages of fourteen and sixteen, to ward off the stigma of "old maid" or "spinster." The latter title came from the tradition of assigning the task of spinning wool for clothing to the oldest daughter in the family, a role that passed to the next unmarried daughter upon the marriage of the first and so on. If a daughter did not marry, she continued to spin for the family. Marrying at eighteen or older was a late marriage and within a breath of the dreaded "old maid" title.

If a sweeping broom brushed over the feet of an unmarried girl, she was at an even greater risk of never marrying. This belief tied into the wedding practice of "jumping the broom," in which case the broom should be *below* the feet of the young woman and never on top.

Weddings never took place on Friday, in honor of Good Friday when Christ was crucified. It was said no good things could happen on a Friday. The tradition of "something old, something new, something borrowed, and something blue" originated with the Scotch-Irish.

Something old gave the new couple a tangible link to their lineage and ancestors. Something new was usually a newly made handcrafted gift such as a handkerchief or the bride's dress, into which good wishes and hopes of fertility were woven by the seamstress(es) who created it. Something borrowed came from a friend or relative who had a happy marriage and lent a personal item to the bride in hopes of passing along their own good fortune in love and marriage. Blue warded off evil, such as the "haint blue" ceilings on many porches, especially of funeral homes; hence "something blue" protected the new couple from misfortune.

Throughout her upbringing, a young girl usually had a "hope chest," which held her "hopes" of a happy marriage. In this chest or trunk, she would store items for her marriage, such as linens and household goods. Often, a girl's mother provided the hope chest when the girl came of age, usually with a few starter items in it. A common addition to the hope chest was a handmade quilt sewn in a wedding ring pattern. Like the wedding dress, the local women produced the quilt with each stitch imbued with good wishes for a happy marriage. Some regions held the tradition that production of the quilt began when the couple announced their engagement and must be completed by the wedding day. The quilt would then take a minimum of nine months to create, thereby assuring that the couple was not marrying because the girl was "in trouble" (pregnant). In these areas, marrying without the wedding quilt brought a stigma to the relationship. If the bride happened to be pregnant at the time of the wedding, the stigma was lessened because the pregnancy had not been the instigator of the engagement and happened within the period of betrothal after the couple pledged to one another.

Presbyterian minsters were rare, primarily due to the rampant persecution of this faith in Ulster, resulting in the British crown declaring their clergy to be invalid. One could not simply receive a calling and become a Presbyterian minister. They must be ordained by the official church, and without churches in the Appalachians, ordinations were uncommon. After the Great Awakenings, a traveling minister could marry a couple, but it was difficult to plan a ceremony because the camp meetings were impromptu events. Word would reach a village that a camp meeting was coming through based on where the camp meeting was previously. This meant that couples often had to wait for quite some time for their wedding. A community elder or head of the clan could conduct a wedding ceremony not ordained by the church, and provided the couple cohabitated for seven years or longer, the union was recognized as an "irregular marriage," sometimes called a "common-law marriage."

After the wedding, a rowdy party called a "charivari" (pronounced by hill folk as "SHivə'rē") took place, involving a great deal of alcohol, ribald joking, dancing, and music. This bawdy reception culminated with the crowd putting the wedding couple to bed and then banging pots and pans and making all sorts of noise to conceal the sounds of their lovemaking as they consummated the marriage.

Healing

In the 1940s, Vance Randolph, a historian and folklorist, spent more than twenty-five years documenting all aspects of life in the Ozarks, and he wrote that yarb doctors were, "brother to the witch and close cousin to the preacher." In his famous book *Ozark Magic and Folklore*, he provides eyewitness descriptions of healing practices used by granny doctors that many modern patients would likely find unpalatable.

The use of cow manure, spider webs, burned alum, pulverized buckeye skins, kerosene, and turpentine for the treatment of a persistent toothache might give patients pause in our time. For healers using easily available resources and finding good results with these cures when no other medical care was available, a pharmacopeia such as this constituted standard operating procedures in treating the sick and injured.

As medical science explores the veracity of healing techniques from this time and area, the reasons why granny doctors were so successful in treating their patients become clear. White willow bark, which a yarb doctor would tell you to chew on to ease the pain of a headache, is the active ingredient in aspirin. Grannies used black cohosh or pennyroyal to induce menstruation, to cause a miscarriage, or to expel the remains of a lost pregnancy. We now know these herbs to be strong uterine stimulants and, when used in appropriate dosages, powerful abortifacients. Chewing on a sprig of mint soothes an irritable stomach, and is now a component in many over-the-counter antacids.

Although the herbs used by the granny women to heal are common to the point that the untrained eye might call them weeds, it is important to keep in mind that what can heal can also harm. It is said that the only difference between medicine and poison is the dosage; part of the skill these healers possessed was the wisdom of how much of what to use when treating a patient. Home medicine is not a practice for the uneducated novice, and extensive research is important before implementing the healing opportunities afforded by the land.

From our educated perspective, we must avoid the rather arrogant presumption that those who practiced (or practice) Granny Magic do so from a position of ignorance or lack of wisdom. In recent years, homeopathic and natural healing interests forced regimented Western medicine to reevaluate their inherent rejection of non-pharmaceutical treatments. As this exploration grows, there is little doubt that we will see the increased legitimacy of the cures used hundreds of years ago.

Certain scriptures contain powerful words of healing, and were chanted repeatedly during healing sessions. Psalms 3 was for backaches and headaches, Psalms 4 was for good luck, Psalms 16 turned friends into enemies and sorrow into joy, Psalms 23 provided visions or dreams for direction, Psalms 41 stopped slander, and Psalms 150 induced gratitude.

As was common practice for the cunning-folk of the old country, the colloquial names given to herbs used for healing and charming might throw off their modern counterparts. "Devil's Dung" was asafetida. "Puke Weed" was the name given to lobelia. Wild ginger, great for stomach upsets, was called "Monkey Jugs." Rue was "Fairy Flute," and calamus/sweet flag was "Moon Root." The friendly and versatile plantain had the odious name of "Snake Weed."

Birth

The mystery of pregnancy and birth had its own cache of beliefs and practices. In the 1700s–1800s, the number one cause of death for women was childbirth or complications of pregnancy. The child mortality rate (birth to five years old) for this area and time is estimated at approximately 40%, mostly due to poor nutrition in expectant mothers resulting in "failure to thrive syndrome," which set in once the child was born and no longer fully fed by the mother's own nutritional stores. A concoction of whole cream boiled with sugar was the common supplement for a failure to thrive baby, and while the idea of such a high fat, high glucose treatment might make the modern purist wince, one must consider that colostrum, the substance that sustains babies and encourages them to nurse while the mother's milk comes in postpartum, is also high in fat and sugar.

From just past puberty through menopause, women conceived often, and if fertile, had many babies, with each birth presenting a real and present danger for both mother and child. Birth control was uncommon, and what herbal contraceptive methods existed were largely ineffective, such as herb-soaked sponges placed in the vagina, or dangerous, such as herbal abortifacients taken internally. Subsequently, families were large, with multiple generations living communally within one dwelling. Long after the rest of the country modernized their dwellings, homes in the Appalachians continued to have no running water or electricity.

The words "pregnant" or "pregnancy" were rarely used and instead terms such as "in the family way," "with child," "in trouble" (if unmarried), "up th' duff," or "wi' a bairn" identified the newly pregnant woman throughout Appalachian history.

A granny midwife must know how to manage both the easy birth and the one with complications, such as an umbilical cord wrapping around the baby's neck. Expectant mothers were encouraged not to raise their arms over their head, because this motion was erroneously thought to wrap the cord around the baby's neck.

Premature separation of the placenta, causing excessive bleeding of mother and baby, is an unfortunate side effect of maternal malnourishment. Pregnant women carried a jasper stone in their pockets to prevent excessive bleeding during birth.

A belief among both granny midwives and traditional doctors of the time was that if a woman's amniotic membranes ruptured before the labor began, she would have a "dry birth" marked by increased pain. We now know that while rupture of the membranes removes the cushion from between the baby's head and the woman's cervix and usually speeds up the process of labor, a dry birth does not actually exist, because the amniotic membranes continue to produce fluid until they leave the body with the afterbirth.

A baby who emerged from the mother's body with the amniotic membranes intact and covering the face was said to be born "with the caul" or "with a veil." The membranes are easily ruptured by the midwife with a quick pinch, resulting in a pressurized gush of fluid as it releases, followed by the quick birth of the baby. A child born with the caul was believed to have "the sight," a term meaning the child possessed psychic abilities and would likely be tapped later as a seer for the community.

Women were careful not to overeat certain foods during pregnancy lest they "mark" their babies with a birthmark. "Strawberry" birthmarks supposedly came from eating an overabundance of the fruit. The common deficiency of vitamin C could cause increased cravings for strawberries and citrus. A "port wine stain" birthmark came supposedly from a pregnant woman drinking any kind of reddish colored alcohol, like elderberry wine or blackberry wine, in pregnancy. Marking could also occur if an animal frightened a pregnant woman. Children who were born marked might be considered holy, cursed, or perfectly normal, depending on the marking.

Newborns wore "navel bands," also called "belly bands," to prevent umbilical hernias or a "rupture," as well as to keep the area around the navel stump cleaner.

A granny midwife would "read" the afterbirth, not only to check the back of the placenta to verify it emerged intact without pieces remaining inside to cause hemorrhage, but also as a divinatory device to determine how many children the woman would ultimately bear. Lumps inside the umbilical cord as it constricted after birth could show not only how many children she would birth, but how many miscarriages she would suffer.

Many techniques existed for pain management in birth, such as placing a knife under the bed to cut the pain or having the laboring woman hold or wear an article of clothing belonging to the man who fathered the baby. Massage, acupressure, and frequent repositioning of the birthing woman also helped offset the pain.

Many divinatory practices predicted the gender of an unborn baby. Tying the woman's wedding ring to a strand of her hair and holding it over her belly created a pendulum effect. If the ring swung back and forth, it meant she carried a boy, and a circular motion indicated the baby was a girl. Traditionally, if a pregnant woman held a young baby on her lap, the baby would relax and snuggle closer to her if her unborn baby was of the opposite gender and would become restless if her unborn baby was of the same gender. A baby carried high in the ribs was a girl and if the pregnancy rode low against the pubic bone, it was a boy. A pregnancy with forward prominence was a girl and a wide pregnancy was a boy.

Birth control was rare, due to the need for many children in a family to provide more working hands, and also because of the danger inherent in most contraceptive methods of the time. Granny doctors offered ways to discourage conception if a woman wished to have a "break" in her annual child-bearing or, for whatever reason, sought to avoid pregnancy. Treatments such as tansy and pennyroyal proved unreliable and even dangerous if used without supervision, and as such, a granny doctor experienced in herbal treatments and gynecological and obstetrical care could literally mean the difference between life and death for a woman.

The overall success and subsequent validation of much of Granny Magic does not mean that their procedures were flawless or that all were conducive to good health. It was common, for instance, for a midwife to pick up a newborn by the heels and shake it roughly to keep it from being "liver growed," a condition in which the liver was thought to attach to the abdominal wall. Now it is known not only that this condition does not exist, but that forcing a newborn infant's hips to support the full weight of its body after being curled into a fetal position for its entire prenatal life can cause hip displacement and severe joint trauma.

A cure for a baby who "had its days and nights mixed up," meaning it slept through the day and was awake at night, involved rolling the child into a towel or blanket, then pulling forcefully on the towel to quickly unwind the baby. Not only is this completely ineffective, since a baby's sleep schedule is established well before birth, but like the previous treatment, such behavior can cause grievous injury. Given some of these procedures, one must wonder if the high child mortality rate might also relate to the cures themselves as much as the environmental factors.

Death

Strongly superstitious, the mountain people had a fascination with death and graveyards; therefore many traditional charms and spells include the use of graveyard dirt, as well as the guidance of ancestral guides and visions, interpreted as guardian angel contact or visions sent from God as depicted in the Bible.

As much as granny women guided the hill folk through birth, they also ushered them into death, managing both hospice care and funeral preparation for the dead and dying. Some even conducted the death rites for the deceased.

Since there were no churches, funerals took place in the cemetery after a "lying in," when family "sat up with the dead" until they were buried. During this time, friends and loved ones could come view the body of the deceased, called a "lych," (liCH) and say their goodbyes. A primary reason for the "sitting up" part of sitting up with the dead was to keep away rodents that threatened to gnaw at the lych if it were left unattended.

Embalming with chemicals did not begin until after the Civil War, and much later in these mountain communities. With no methods of body preservation, the burial happened quickly after the death. Tradition stated that spirits lingered along any trail used to transport the lych to the cemetery, so to keep the spirit population contained to one place, all mourners walked to the cemetery using a single path for any burial.

One tradition from 18th and 19th century Scotland that carried over to some areas of Appalachia is that of "sin eating." A sin eater attended to the dying and recently dead by reciting an incantation, then eating food laid upon or passed over the lych, thereby taking into their own body the unconfessed and unforgiven sins committed by the dead or dying person.

Taking in the sins of the dying condemned the sin eater's soul to eternal damnation, so when or if the identity of the sin eater was known, they faced shunning from the community. In many cases, the sin eater arrived wearing a black cloak and hood like that of an executioner, keeping their identity secret from everyone in the village to avoid the stigma. The role of the sin eater was often passed generationally within a single family in the community.

In exchange for the unburdening of the departing soul, the sin eater received the meal, which may have been only a piece of bread, and a fee of one to two dollars, which was a significant amount in the context of the time and circumstances.

When a death occurred, any mirrors in the home were immediately covered with black cloth to prevent the recently deceased from looking back at the living through the reflection. Another tradition from this area was that any clocks in the house were stopped at the minute of death and not restarted until after the burial.

Witches, Curses & Other Mystical Things

There were no new age theologies such as spiritual awakening, personal actualization, enlightenment, astral travel, or any transcendental realm other than Heaven. A major turning point in mountain spirituality was the concept of being "saved," introduced by the camp meetings of the Great Revival or Great Awakenings of the late 1800s. Until then, people did not experience a religious turning point when they were suddenly one of God's children or transformed into a Christian. They were those things from the time they were born and lived as such.

The Cherokee and the Scotch-Irish shared a belief in the non-human entities such as fairies, ghosts, demons, spirits, and angels. Frequent offerings of milk, honey, and sugar water kept these supernatural beings satisfied and happy so they did not inflict any mischief on humans.

Another belief shared by these two cultures was that natural openings such as caves were "in between" places that served as portals to other worlds. Meadows with large crops of the fragrant herb meadowsweet were believed to be home to the fairies, and if one chanced to go to sleep while amid the herb field, they might not make it back to the "real" world. A fairy ring was a natural formation of flowers, foliage, or raised earth in the rough or even concise shape of a circle. The fairies were thought to play within these ring shapes.

Folk stories out of the mountains in the Eastern United States demonstrate the use of kinship names and personification processes for natural occurrences, with examples such as Father Time, Grandmother Moon, Jack Frost, Mother Nature, and Spider Grandmother. This reflects their strong connection and vulnerability to the cycles of nature, and although we would view this as animism, they did not. To them, it was creating relatability to the natural cycles and occurrences.

In her books *In a Graveyard at Midnight* and *Mountain Magick* (the same book published under different titles), Edain McCoy distinguishes between "Witch" (a person dedicated to nature-based magical practices who works with natural energy to produce supernatural results) and the Appalachian definition of "witch" (a person in league with the Christian devil who works to harm and introduce supernaturally created misfortune into the life of its victims) by using the capitalized and lowercase W. As she points out, although the words are the same, the meaning imparted by the user is completely different. The people we cover in the scope of this book had no concept of a Witch and knew only of witches, closer to their portrayal in classic fairy tales. I follow her example in this text because quite frankly, it works well.

Both Ms. McCoy and I identify ourselves as Witches and intend no disparagement to our colleagues in that field; however, to present the most accurate representation of the beliefs of the Scotch-Irish in Appalachia and the Ozarks, we must view the world through their eyes.

The management of aggressive witches also fell under the purview of the power doctor, who assisted those who fell victim to the evil doings of a witch—things like hexing, or the terror of Appalachian and Ozark people, the "witch ball."

These balls, made of beeswax mixed with hair from cows or horses, and when possible, the hair and nail trimmings of the victim, were hurled at a person to curse them and were said to render a person gravely ill, cause them to faint, or bring instant death. Created by a witch at the behest of another or because she was just that ornery, being in concert with the devil and all, these wax curse balls were flung at the victim or flicked off the thumb and they could, according to legend, travel miles to reach their intended target. They could alternately drop unseen into a pocket or slip into the corner of a bedroom or an automobile. If the witch ball did not hit its intended target, tradition warned that it would return to hit the witch who made it. This caused witches to be highly motivated in making certain the ball reached their intended victim. Goomer doctors knew how to uncross someone hit by a witch ball, provided the victim did not drop dead on the spot the second the witch ball struck them.

A curse could be undone or deflected by winding a lock of your hair and your own nail clippings around a stick from your own yard then tying the assembly together with a red string. The person requiring protection carried this defensive talisman until the threat passed.

The staunch Christian identification of the Appalachian and Ozark people of this time was absolute, and to be a Pagan, or worse, a witch, was about the worst thing anyone could imagine. They spoke of witches in the harshest of terms and feared them outright as the cause of nearly all maladies, whether medical, agricultural, or related to animal husbandry. If the cows stopped producing milk, then a witch must have cursed the cows. If a person became ill and no diagnosis or cure came to the fore, a witch must have cursed the person. If the crops withered in the sun? Witch. Any misadventure or misfortune likely started with a witch.

And yet, they would never imagine that *their* witch would do such a thing, and therein lies the irony of the situation. Nearly every village, holler, and mountaintop had its own "witch." To the experience and conviction of the hill people, witches shape-shifted, ate children, consorted with the devil, had powers of invisibility, and could single-handedly cripple a village … "except for *our* witch, Granny So-and-So, who is the kindest, sweetest, most capable, God-fearing Christian woman you'd ever want to meet and I would trust her with my life." Witches were *bad* and the source of tremendous fear. They were the go-to explanation for any calamity … *but not our witch.*

In fact, any book on Appalachian and Ozark Granny Magic invariably includes a large section on charms to protect against witchcraft, sorcery, and crossing. This reflects the black and white nature of the mountain belief system. There was no gray and no ambiguity. People and circumstances were "good" or "bad" without room for interpretation. In general, a witch fell soundly into the "bad" categorization, but "our" witch, through her kind actions and capable practices, earned her way into "good" standing.

Every action, every experience, and every natural expression came from God or came from the Devil, with nothing in between. All injuries, illnesses, and misfortunes had a spiritual cause and meant that God was displeased with the victim or that a witch had cursed them, sometimes at the behest of another person and sometimes because witches were just bad people with nothing better to do. Conversely, a healthy person who encountered minimal misfortune had God's blessings upon them.

More Magical Beliefs & Practices

While *we* may refer to the practices of the people of the Ozarks and Appalachians as "Granny Magic" or "folk magic," they would not do so and did not describe their healing or spirituality in these terms or any other, for that matter. They did not identify as Pagans or, God forbid, as Witches, nor did they even identify in that era as Scotch-Irish. We assigned labels to them in modern times, but they saw no need to brand this part of their everyday life. Geographically, they referred to themselves by the state in which they lived rather than from where they originated. They were "Virginians" or "Tennessee people."

Shoes carried magical significance, especially since they were a luxury that many could not afford. The belief of the time was that, even with shoe ownership at a premium, one must always be careful about wearing the shoes worn another person since the magic of "walk a mile in my shoes" could come to life and impart the fortune or misfortune of the previous wearer onto the current one. Most people only wore shoes previously worn by other members of the family or by close friends. Clothing also carried the imprint of the experiences of the previous wearer, so it was bad luck to wear the wedding dress of a bride whose marriage was unhappy or to wear the hat of a man who did not live (or die) well.

The types of wood burned on the hearth each brought a specific influence into the home it warmed. Pine and cedar encouraged a good harvest. Birch brought joy and peace to the home. Elm offered protection from supernatural threats, while oak protected the home from physical danger such as natural disasters. A broom laid across the hearth prevented the good fortune of the home from escaping up the chimney and kept bad luck or evil entities from entering the home through the chimney.

A type of focused magical work, much like Hoodoo doll babies or poppets, happened with corn dollies. These human-shaped figures, fashioned out of corn husks, worked well for sympathetic magic, inflicting a curse, or working healing from a distance. It could also draw in a husband or prevent one from wandering with the use of correct incantations and herbs, and then subsequent burning.

Washing your door with a mixture of vinegar and your own urine purified and protected the entire home. This is reminiscent of the use of Four Thieves Vinegar in Hoodoo tradition and explains why being full of "piss and vinegar" was a desirable quality.

Mirrors were rare to find in Appalachia and Ozark homes due to their cost. The tradition that breaking a mirror brought seven years bad luck addresses the value of the item and the fact that it would take the profits of seven harvests to replace one. The person who broke the mirror must always bury the shards in a graveyard to keep the spirits of all those who ever gazed into it from coming through into the present time. Since most mirrors were family heirlooms passed through many generations, there could be a flood of spirits ready to come through.

There were no magical tools as we think of them in modern Pagan life. The same knife was used to cut an umbilical cord as was used to peel potatoes. Life was, above all, practical, and all tools must be multipurpose and useful in many ways. Tools were handmade and were simple, ordinary, and easily available to the user.

Over time and with the continued influx of African American migrants moving northward and settling into the mountain regions, religious and spiritual expressions in the Ozark and Appalachian area came to include full-body baptisms, foot washing, chanting, preaching, and congregational shouting. These components also came in during the Methodist and Baptist camp meetings that transient ministers from the South brought through the area.

Although as previously mentioned, most people in this area were illiterate, and traditions and practices were usually communicated orally, there were a few exceptions to this rule. *The Old Farmer's Almanac* first went into annual publication in 1792. The periodical included weather predictions, anecdotes, and planting guides for the coming year, and was of tremendous value to the mountain people.

Most homes had a family Bible, even if no one in the house could read it. Important dates were noted in the logged pages by those who could write, and significant documents might be pressed between the pages.

One of the few books from the time that documented true mountain folk magic was *Long Lost Friend,* a collection of 190 charms used for everything from crop management to animal care to weather magic to healing. Written by German printer and bookseller, John George Hohman, *Long Lost Friend* was the consummate poor people's guide to problem-solving and crisis management using Pow-wow charms and chants. So revered was this work that, like the Holy Bible, the book itself was said to possess magical powers.

Some historians claim that nearly all homes had a copy of *Long Lost Friend* shoved into some drawer somewhere in the house, but more recent estimations insist that its use was not as widespread as was previously believed. It is hard to track usage of the book, because its charms and chants were so close to what was then considered to be the occult that good Christian folk would often swear they never possessed such a thing, only to later admit that they might have an old copy around that someone left there.

When one identifies magic as the manipulation of energy to achieve a desired effect, the power of folk magic is undeniable. While those who practiced and benefited from it would not lay claim to magical properties inherent in the techniques used, taken objectively and by definition, it is some of the most powerful spellwork our country has seen.

Simply stated, these people had charms, spells, chants, and wards *for everything*. Unfortunately, a great deal of this localized information is now lost to us due to the lack of written transference. As increasing influences of modern life slowly integrated into the remote mountain communities where Granny Magic flourished, the reliance on folk magic for problem solving plummeted. As fewer people used folk magic, the practices fell away into history, many never to be seen again.

─── 12 ───
Appalachian and Ozark Granny Magic Today

Of the three folk magic traditions presented here, Granny Magic is arguably the most obscure and over time has faded almost into oblivion. There are a few revivalists who work to keep the historical practices alive, many of whom have authentic ancestral ties to the traditions.

Anna Wess is an award-winning essayist and storyteller from the foothills of the Appalachian Mountains in southwestern Virginia, and is a practicing granny. Her online blog, Appalachian Ink (appalachianink.net/), evokes the essence of Appalachian living in beautiful prose and nostalgic sentiment. Her most popular work is her essay called "The Last of the Granny Witches," in which she sums up life as a granny by saying, "We are a mystery as old as these hills themselves, and it doesn't take much figuring to know that we are enigmas of intentional design and destiny."

Her words are grounded in the memory of Appalachian folk magic, and she translates the experience into modern life in a uniquely poetic fashion.

One of the most famous modern-day granny witches is the self-identified forensic folklorist, Byron Ballard, who intertwines Granny Magic with Hoodoo. Ballard is an active healer and practitioner who laments the appropriation of hill folk magic by outsiders, calling it "cultural strip-mining."

Ballard is not the only voice decrying appropriation and even contamination of a pure tradition that survived for so long specifically because of its isolation in remote, inaccessible areas until technology caught up. I have personally heard the grumbling of granny witches who complain that modern practitioners "wiccanize" a path that is Christian in origin, thereby diluting the purity of the work and insulting the history that created the system of folk magic. The relatively new practice of cherry-picking individual components from various paths to create a composite practice is widespread in the magical community, but distinctly unpopular with those who feel a tradition should remain intact and cohesive for all its followers. Others feel that only those who have a cultural, geographic, or genetic bond with a folk magic path should hold entitlement to its practice, and anything else is appropriation at best and exploitation at worst.

A public proponent of blended paths is author Orion Foxwood, an avid and experienced teacher of many traditions, including Witchcraft, Faery Seership Tradition, Southern Folk Magic, and Hoodoo. His books, *The Flame in the*

Cauldron: A Book of Old-Style Witchery and *The Candle and the Crossroads: A Book of Appalachian Conjure and Southern Root-Work,* specifically address his experiences growing up in the magical Appalachian Mountains and include many of his charms and rituals, as well as his own musings about working in these fields.

Foxwood has a strong following and is beloved for his amiable and relatable writing style as well as his lectures on various forms of folk magic and his other areas of expertise. He has, however, drawn marked criticism for his melting pot approach to the various magical practices he embraces.

Unlike his predecessors, Foxwood does not hesitate to identify as a Witch and blends his folk magic practices with Hoodoo and elements of Wicca and Witchcraft. Byron Ballard also identifies freely as a Witch, even to the point of titling her blog My Village Witch.

Wess, on the other hand, while not directly maligning those who are practicing Witches, eschews the word herself, saying, "This ain't witchcraft. It's wildcraft" (Wess 2016).

Many of those who identify with Appalachian or Ozark folk magic in current times also integrate Hoodoo and European Pagan practices such as Wicca, Ásatrú, or Druidism into their belief systems and magical work. Some identify as Christian while others do not, leading those who are purists to insist that one cannot practice "real" Granny Magic without embracing Christianity.

The Scotch-Irish were thrifty and resourceful, using the techniques and tools that were available to them. Granny magic was a living religion, and the reason it persisted into modern time was its ability to adapt and use all available resources.

Considering the overlapping modalities between Granny Magic and Hoodoo, the impact of Cherokee herbal knowledge, and the demonstrated ability to weave modern concepts such as umbrellas and trains into the fabric of Granny Magic, it is hard to imagine that as the outside world reached the isolated Appalachian and Ozark people, they would not integrate all available resources into their practice. Their way was to use what was available and what worked, and there appears to be no historical resistance to shared information. As such, the idea of incorporating components of other magical paths into the Granny Magic structure does not seem as invasive, particularly when one approaches it from the perspective that a path that does not evolve and adapt eventually becomes unsustainable and dies out.

The practice of lay midwifery has continued in Appalachia and the Ozarks longer than anywhere else in the United States. Now called "direct entry midwives," trained professionals still provide home birth options to expectant mothers throughout the country, carrying on the traditions of our foremothers.

Appalachian and Ozark Granny Magic remains with us in our nursery rhymes, our superstitions, and our "old wives' tales." Time spent in geographical regions closest to the Appalachians and Ozarks reveals a richer concentration of residual practices that still season day-to-day life of the people who live there.

More than any of the other folk magic systems presented in this book, Granny Magic is the closest to full extinction. There are those few dedicated practitioners mentioned above who keep the oil lights burning for the tradition, working hard to preserve the healing and conjuring practices that were so vital to those long-ago clan structures. As with any practice, there are those who continue the old ways outside of the spotlight of the internet and book publication. There are grandmothers and grandfathers still living who remember these times and these ways or remember their parents healing with common items. These stories need to be recorded and preserved.

The woman in my hometown in Kentucky who lived by the railroad and enchanted her animals, including chickens, cows, ducks, pigs, and others to live in her house is now dead. She was the woman everyone said was a witch, just like the shape-shifting, witch ball hurling, curse-wielding witches from those mountain communities. She was not even *our* witch, but just *a* witch, and therefore utterly suspect. When I was maybe five or six years old in the early 1960s, my mother told me about the time the woman got angry with the railroad company because her cow got onto the tracks near her home and the train hit it. She greased the tracks with lard, cursed the train, and it derailed. My mother is dead now, so there is no one to ask about this anymore, but even at the tender age of five or six, I did not believe that the woman was a witch, because witches weren't real. The story is gone except in my head and now on these pages, but oh how I would love to hear that story one more time by someone who was there.

I would give anything to talk to my grandfather, dead of black lung disease since 1967, about water witching and dowsing. I would love to hear my grandmother talk about sharecropping and home births and her unexpected set of twins, one of which was my mother. Like the woman who cursed the train, those stories are irretrievable to me now.

Perhaps yours are not. Find them and preserve them before they blink out like the last firefly of the year.

How did Granny Magic all but disappear in less than a century? Technology and urban society eventually found its way into the deepest recesses of the Appalachians. Many of the people who live there are still impoverished, but there are roads and vehicles making mainstream society more accessible. Even the poorest communities now have hospitals, churches, schools, and the influence of commerce and industry. Money is commerce now, whereas in the 1800s–1900s, business was done through barter or a handshake.

The heart of Appalachian Granny Magic still beats, but it is weak, and the tradition lives on more out of nostalgia and anachronistic wistfulness than for the fervent need it filled before. Government-funded health care now meets the medical needs of those who cannot afford health insurance, and the remote mountain areas are now almost all parishes for at least one church, usually more, to address the spiritual needs of a congregation. People do not need one another quite as much as they did in the Appalachians in the 1700s–1800s and even into the 1900s. The interconnectedness is still there in the faint whisper of outsiderism and phrases like the accusing, "Y'all ain't from around here, are ya?"

In Hoodoo, Brujería, and Curanderismo, the cultures from which the folk magic traditions grew all but fought for their continuation and preservation. The mountain people were quick to label themselves according to their new surrounding areas, while Mexican Americans and African Americans kept a tighter hold on their historic cultural identities.

In Appalachia, new generations eagerly broke out of the confines of isolation and integrated into the modern world even as the modern world found Appalachia. Poverty and inaccessibility constructed and encapsulated the Granny Magic practices for hundreds of years, and as those issues resolved or partially resolved, the Granny Magic began to slip away into history.

Granny Magic, as previously stated, developed in isolated pockets of the Appalachians with little networking between communities to create continuity of practice. This disconnectedness from other people practicing similar folk magic was also was likely part of the breakdown of tradition. With only a relative handful of people embracing the traditions of a singular clan, as those people died off, so did the practices.

One of the most critical contributors to the dissolution of Granny Magic, second only to the broadened accessibility to the outside world and the opportunities it presented, is the fact that the people who used and benefitted from Granny Magic saw it as everyday life. It was not special or unique in any way. It was a means to an end, and as other, easier means to achieve that same end presented themselves, there was little interest in preserving the more rudimentary means that had carried them through until then.

For many years, I have had the privilege of interacting with people in the American Pagan communities. Most have heard of Brujería and Hoodoo. Few who are not within the Hispanic culture have heard of Curanderismo, but within that culture, it is well-known and appreciated. A friend of mine just mentioned to me this week that she went on a retreat and received healings from multiple curanderas. Within their cultural construct, Brujería and Curanderismo are thriving and Hoodoo is the Next Big Thing in Paganism, with plenty of books on the shelves to guide the aspiring rootworker, and endless blogs, instructional pages, and teaching videos available online.

Almost no one I speak to has heard of Granny Magic, however. When I lecture on folk magic, I see recognition until I reach the discussion of Mountain Magic. Then the brows furrow, their heads tilt to one side, and a moment of confusion sets in for my audience. As I talk about the tradition further, some folks recognize a few of the various beliefs and superstitions and then they feel a greater sense of relatability. Initially, however, the response is almost universally "Huh?"

When writing this book, I groaned inwardly when my acquisitions editor asked me if I could flesh out the Granny Magic section a bit. I knew I had already exhausted my available resources, but of course I smiled and said, "Surrrrre." In addition to my own firsthand experience, I read the few books available on the subject, including special requesting Edain McCoy's book from Llewellyn for reference, then oh-so-gently shipping it back. I perused blogs and watched You-Tube videos on the Scotch-Irish, looking for new tidbits to share. The fact is that there is just not very much information left out there, partly due to the lack of written documentation over the two hundred plus years of its more blanketed use and partly because of the tradition quickly slipping away.

What I offer to you here is dear to my heart and cherished even more for its scarcity. My hope is that raising awareness of this interesting and nuanced folk magic system kindles some increase in interest and opens new avenues of conversation and information sharing. If you have access to do so, get those stories, share those home cures, and write down those healing and weather charms. They are a sacred part of our history and a precious cache of wisdom.

──── 13 ────
Appalachian and Ozark Charms and Spells

Within the Granny Magic construct, all working served a practical purpose, usually centered around protection on all levels, health concerns, family and marital harmony, and the success and safety of crops and livestock. They rarely addressed the acquisition of riches or abundance except in terms of good luck and good fortune. The scope of life's goals was to marry well and early, have a family of healthy children, maintain a house to shelter that family, develop a skill to support that family, live a good life, and die feeling fulfilled. Aspirations beyond that noble few were frowned upon and considered to be putting on airs.

Protection

Hang basil around any entries into or out of your house to keep the haints away. Plant rosemary around your house for protection from two-legged, four-legged, and six-legged critters. Some herbs work better when cut and others are more effective as they grow. For instance, basil and mint have stronger magical properties after cutting and rosemary is at the height of its power when it is still in the ground.

Carry a branch from a tree struck by lightning for protection. If the branch is large enough, make it into a walking stick for the height of personal protection.

Carry mistletoe in your pocket to ward off lightning strikes. Mistletoe also foretells a marriage proposal in the spring if one is kissed under it during the winter.

Blue glass bottles repel negativity. Place the following items into a blue glass bottle to create a home protection bottle: hair from each person living in the home, ashes from the home's hearth, and dirt from the area next to the front and back steps to the house. Place the blue bottle on the front porch or in a tree in the front yard of the home.

Colored glass itself carries strong magical connotations. Placing multi-colored bottles into tree branches by shoving the branch into the bottle creates a "bottle tree," which is a strong home talisman in the South. Bottle trees convey the color magic properties of the bottle color to protect those who live in the home and to imbue the home with the blessings traditional to those colors.

Removing and Warding Off Curses

Remove a curse by sleeping a full night on a freshly dug grave, especially that of a near relative. This increases the influence and protection of the deceased loved one around you and allows them to pull the curse into the grave with them forevermore.

Bang a nail into the crib post to ward off evil curses. Iron itself is protective, particularly against witches and evil faeries. The nail repels all evil entities and keeps the child safe.

Touch the side of your nose if you see someone giving you the evil eye, and recite Psalm 94 three times to ward off evil sent to you by another person.

Health

Carry a bloodstone to prevent pregnancy loss. A goomer doctor could give a pregnant woman a small medicine bag (called a gris-gris or mojo bag in Hoodoo) to protect her and her unborn child during pregnancy. This could include a bloodstone to prevent miscarriage, a jasper to reduce bleeding in pregnancy and childbirth, and a lock of hair from the mother and from the father to further the good health and protection of the baby.

Give a newborn baby a taste of the ashes from the hearth to prevent crib death. Ashes from a person's home hearth were sacred, and throughout winter it was bad luck for the fire to go out, mostly because people could freeze to death. When the coal or wood fire went out in the spring, it meant the seer or granny had predicted that winter's grip was over for the year. Placing a bit of the hearth ashes on the baby's tongue gave the baby the assurance of continued life and the protection of the entire home.

If you feel a cold coming on, slice an onion and use clean linen strips to bind the slices to the bare bottoms of your feet at night. The onion will draw the cold out of your body through your feet while you sleep.

To cure a wart, draw a drop of blood from the wart and put it on a grain of corn. Feed the corn to a black hen and the wart will go away.

Bury your own hair clippings under a stone in a cemetery to cure headaches. Like a curse, the spirits of the cemetery will pull the head pain into the grave with them to disburse into the earth and plague you no more.

Marriage and Home Life

Twist an apple stem as you recite the alphabet. The letter you speak as the stem breaks away is the first letter of the name of your future spouse.

Throw a cotton pouch filled with basil and rosemary into the hearth fire to bring happiness to the home.

Put a fresh sprig of rosemary under the mattress of your husband to keep him from straying. Burn the rosemary the next day and replace it with a new sprig. Do this for nine straight days. The same charm can work on women if you use mugwort instead of rosemary.

Luck

Put a thrown horseshoe over your front door for luck, but make sure the U points upward so the luck doesn't run out.

Iron provides protection for many disincarnate and aggressive entities.

To carry a rabbit's foot is lucky, but it is not as simple as acquiring any old rabbit's foot. It must be a left hind foot, and you must kill the rabbit in a graveyard on top of a grave on a Friday, unless it is raining. If it happens to be raining at the time, you must do it on a Saturday … even if it is raining on Saturday. Additionally, killing the rabbit must happen within one day of the new moon.

Finding a silver pin on the ground is lucky if you pick up the pin and stick it into your collar or lapel. The rhyme "See a penny, pick it up. All day long you'll have good luck" was originally "See a pin and pick it up …"

Divination, Omens, and Portents

If your left hand itches, you will lose money. If your right hand itches, you will get money.

If a blackbird sits on the roof, someone will die within two weeks. If a blackbird sits on the windowsill, it is bad luck.

If a broom falls over, company is coming.

If smoke moves straight up from a chimney, the weather will clear soon, if it is rainy, foggy, or snowy. If smoke stays close to the roof, it will rain or snow by the next night, unless birds are flying around it. If smoke goes back toward the chimney, the weather will change from what it is at that time.

PART 3

BRUJERÍA AND CURANDERISMO

——— 14 ———
About Brujería
and Curanderismo

With origins in Mexico and Spain, with Native American and Hoodoo influences, Brujería and Curanderismo represent a thriving and often underground magical system existing predominately in the southwestern United States. Like Hoodoo and Granny Magic, Brujería and Curanderismo focus on basic needs, with an emphasis on concepts such as healing, prosperity, love, fertility, retribution, and "a good death."

Whereas Hoodoo is thriving in our current magical culture and Granny Magic has all but died out, Brujería is alive and well, but is quite secreted into the folds of Hispanic and Latin communities. Almost everyone within those social constructs knows where to find the local bruja or curandero, but an outsider new to the environment would rarely see a sign advertising their services.

Unlike Hoodoo and Granny Magic, Brujería and Curanderismo use gender-specific terms to identify those within their practices. Throughout the discussion of this fascinating magical construct, I use the male and female terms interchangeably. A brujo is a male witch and a bruja is a female witch. A curandero is a male healer and a curandera is a female healer. Brujería and Curanderismo are the spiritual practices themselves, representing dark and light sides of the same coin. Both genders fill the same roles in Brujería and Curanderismo.

There are many people who take exception to the idea that Brujería and Curanderismo are similar practices. There are certain distinctions that set them apart, but for the most part, their ambitions are the same and their methods are the same. I identify as a part of both, because I can walk with equal ease and capability in both fields.

Brujería and Curanderismo are not a set of techniques you can learn from a book or the internet. That may well be why there is such a dearth of information out there on Mexican magic. Brujería and Curanderismo are not about memorizing the right spells and reciting incantations in the correct way. This path is not about knowing what herbs to use for healing or what acupressure point to use for pain relief. Certainly all those components are important to the practice, but the primary influence in Brujería and Curanderismo is something that cannot be conveyed through print. *It is a feeling.*

The best way to sum it up is to say that one does not *become* a curandera or a bruja. One *discovers* that one *is* a curandera or a bruja. I *became* a rootworker, and a very competent one. My results in healing and conjuring were consistently good. The calling to Brujería and Curanderismo is a beacon to come home, not an avocation to adopt. There is a traditional saying in Brujería that is, "Once a brujo, always a brujo." My belief is that the "always" of that statement extends not only to the future, but also to the past.

As I learned various techniques from my mentor, the feeling was quite different than it was when I learned to be a rootworker. I was not learning, but *remembering,* even though in this life I had not had those experiences. The many other brujos and curanderos I have met since I began my training all share a story like mine in that respect. Like a sneeze, the feeling is difficult to describe, but you instinctively know what to do when it happens.

When I work with my mentor and other brujas and curanderas, there is an energy flow that binds us together and creates circuits in which the divine power and personal energy, blended with the complimentary energy of the natural products we use, can travel. The erection of that power grid is not something a person can learn academically. It is an experiential process that defies description, and it is within that structure that the real magic of Brujería and Curanderismo happens.

The word *Curanderismo* derives from the Spanish word *curar,* which means "to heal." Curanderismo is a sophisticated process of healing that goes far beyond the management of physical symptoms, to integrate spiritual and psychological components into the scope of treatment. Primary to a curandero's diagnosis, treatment plan, and prognosis of any condition is the evaluation of the whole of a person. In consideration of injury, illness, or misfortune, the curandero performs a careful and detailed examination to ferret out psychological, social, environmental, or spiritual factors that contribute to the client's condition, as well as the obvious physical manifestations of illness.

For the Mexican-Americans who engage a curandera, what we think of as magic—meaning the supernatural components of the healing process—is an integral part of the treatment of the "whole" person. The practitioner treating a woman who seeks out a charm to keep her husband from straying does so with the same evaluative and diagnostic approach they would apply to a man showing symptoms suggesting diabetes. A healer in these traditions views disadvantage and misfortune as part of the multi-leveled network of dis-ease. In curing the person, they consider socio-psychological components into the factors they must address within the treatment process.

In her book 1999 book, *Woman Who Glows in the Dark*, curandera Elena Avila says, "Curanderismo teaches that it is not enough to diagnose a physical problem, as so many modern medical doctors do, without also looking at what is going on in the heart and soul of the patient."

Curanderismo is a vocation specific to healing on multiple levels and is culturally accepted and appreciated. Brujería, on the other hand, is magic, and never represents itself as anything else, even though healing is involved in that process as well. Brujería shares the perspective of Curanderismo in that it treats the client as a systematic whole. Brujos simply do so from the other side. A curandera sees a patient displaying symptoms in the physical world and considers whether there is also a spiritual or psychological component. The bruja sees a client displaying spiritual symptoms and considers whether there also is a physical or psychological component.

Most Mexican-Americans who work from a traditional perspective view the bruja and brujo with disdain, rather than showing them societal distinction and acceptance afforded to practitioners of Curanderismo. As with Granny Magic, a witch is not seen as a Pagan person who heals with herbs and engages supernatural energies through spellwork to achieve the desired outcome. That is, in fact, what a curandero does, almost to the letter. And yet neither a curandera nor her clients would ever dare consider what she does to be Brujería. A bruja is mistrusted and often ostracized, but is the last resort for those in crisis who are unable to find solutions elsewhere.

Most Mexican and Mexican-American cultures think of the brujos as those who possess the same powers to access the supernatural or divine energies that the curanderos engage to heal, but who do so with the full intention of inflicting evil and misfortune upon others. There is a presumption of malice and lack of moral or ethical restriction assigned to the bruja. This denigration seems to come from the willingness of the bruja to go to extreme measures if necessary on behalf of their client. The ability and willingness to do so often generate the idea that the motives of the brujo are always malicious, cold-hearted, or otherwise vicious.

The brujas and brujos I know, including myself, focus on determining the outcome most likely to improve the quality of life of the client and work aggressively to achieve that outcome. I tell my clients that we must approach Brujería as we do any medicine. We start at the lowest dose of the safest "medicine" and then increase the dosage or shift to a stronger "medicine" as needed. Another phrase I often use is "Don't bring a gun to a knife fight," meaning to tailor your magical firepower to the situation rather than wading in with guns blazing. Knowing what resources and techniques to use demands a complete evaluation of the client and their circumstances, with the same degree of care and discernment that the curandera would use.

People engage a bruja when there is no other hope, often under the cover of night, in secret to avoid others seeing that they did so. You do not speak to her if you see her on the street. You train your eyes straight ahead and cross to the other side if possible, even if she saved your life, your marriage, your job, or your children the week before. The bruja solves your problems for you and you always make certain your accounts are settled with her on the spot. As a bruja, I always tell my client that their account is settled and they owe me nothing once their bill is paid. This reassures them that they are not indebted to me on any level.

While the brujo is maligned, despised, and feared, the curandero is loved, revered, and more importantly, legitimized. Both use roots, herbs, eggs, fruits, stones, crystals, candles, animal and botanical products, and divinatory tools to help their clients. Both pray with and for their clients and use energy movement to create change in their clients' lives. Both access supernatural forces from "beyond the veil" to intervene with and influence their client's travails and desires.

Although there are still brujas and curanderas working throughout the United States, the practice is diminishing as modern health care choices become more available to the average Mexican-American.

When I began public practice as a bruja in my botánica in Roseville, California, a few years ago, I asked a dear friend of mine who is Hispanic if she felt I should use my title of "curandera," rather than identifying as a "bruja," to avoid the negative connotations some of the Hispanic community held against the brujas. She shrugged and said, "Those who matter will know and those who do not know do not matter" and advised that I stay with the label of bruja, which I mostly do. My personal blending of Brujería with Hoodoo also allows me to use the more generalized term *rootworker.*

Curanderismo is a set of ancient Mesoamerican medical and ritual practices that create proactive physical and spiritual healing on all levels. In modern parlance, we would call what Curanderismo does, "holistic healing." Brujería is a systemized magical practice that uses rituals, herbs, and magical tools to access the supernatural world in such a way as to create physical, mental, emotional, sexual, social, or spiritual change that manifests in our material world.

———— 15 ————
Types of Practitioners

As previously mentioned, the Spanish language uses gender identification in the words that represent the magical practitioners of these two paths: the *curandero* (male), the *curandera* (female), the *brujo* (male), and the *bruja* (female). In each instance, the males and females perform the same services, with the exception of the *partera*, which is a curandera who is also a midwife. The partera is almost always female.

Curandera or curandero is not a title one claims, such as saying, "I am now a rootworker." Most curanderas think of themselves simply as "healers" until the community in which they work identifies them as a "curandera" out of respect for their successes. Likewise, in the Granny Magic traditions, a woman does not usually think of herself as "Granny so-and-so." The village bestows the title of "Granny" on her out of respect for a lifetime of healing and care provided.

One can *study* Curanderismo, but does not refer to one-self as a curandera until the title is bestowed upon them. Even then, many elder curanderas do not use the term in self-iden-tification, preferring to identify as a "healer" for the duration of their practice, which is typically lifelong.

A bruja or brujo, on the other hand, is a personal iden-tification rather than a title. It can also be an accusation. Objectively, it is merely the Spanish word for witch. An apt comparison is that the curandera is the kindly, healing woman who knows aggressive means for combatting illness on all levels and the brujo is the weird, reclusive guy who lives at the edge of the village and has solutions to your prob-lems if you are brave enough to seek him out. Many are, but are bane to admit it. The bruja is often the community's best kept secret.

The real distinction between bruja and curandera came about due to the influence of the Catholic Church. Identifica-tion as a healer was not only acceptable, but admirable to the Church. Anyone who presented as a witch, however, was ma-ligned and prosecuted. The smear campaign against witches that originated in Europe migrated to Mexico with the Span-ish conquistadors and infiltrated the culture as the Catholic Church took deep hold of the spiritual interests of the new Spanish lands. The Spanish migration also brought with it grimoires of Spanish occultists, which found their way into the hands of those who persisted in identifying as witches. The alchemical and ceremonial information included in the grimoires shifted the Conjure styles of the brujas so that their methods of healing and divination became less familiar to the masses. Between the denigration of witches by the now prevalent Catholic Church and the new and unfamiliar practices incorporated into the bruja's practices, the stage was set for a full rejection of Brujería.

Mythologies of brujas as shape-shifters, baby-eaters, and hex-throwers permeate the culture. This historical vilification created a strong polarization between the image of the bruja and the curandera, with curandera emerging as the more socially accepted title. Whereas the bruja was akin to a malevolent figure of urban legend, capable not only of extreme supernatural powers but also of profound evil intention, the curandera was a benevolent and sacred healer.

Most curanderas and curanderos work in general practice and are called a *curandero total* or a *curandera total;* however, some branch off into specialty fields, such as the partera. *Yerberos* specialize in herbal healing. *Hueseros* work with human skeletal ailments, setting of bones, and performing physical therapy for muscles and tendons. *Oracionistas* heal using focused prayer and s*obadores* use massage techniques. All fall under the umbrella of the curandera.

Curanderos work on three different levels and may specialize in one level or use any combination of the three. These levels are the material level (*nivel material*), the mental level (*nivel mental*), and the spiritual level (*nivel espiritual*).

The material level, *nivel material,* addresses the outward manifestation of symptoms, such as the use of herbs in poultices, tinctures, or teas, as well as ritual incantations and physical objects and tools to cure disease, misfortune, or injury. This type of healing utilizes the energies inherent in the objects, the vibratory levels of certain colors, and the application of natural resources to cure the symptoms that are present.

Curanderos who work on the mental level, the *nivel mental,* are less common than those who work primarily on the material level. These healers may work remotely rather than in a "hands-on" capacity, using the client's name and sometimes the date of birth as a focal point to direct energy toward the resolution of their condition. They can work to dominate the thoughts of another to overcome a pervasive and destructive habit or to change behavior that affects the quality of life of the patient or those around them. This level of healing involves extensive training.

The spiritual level, *nivel espiritual,* involves more of a shamanistic or mediumship approach, with the healer connecting to the spirit world to diagnose, cure, and/or influence the future course of events. They can find lost or stolen items, name the perpetrator of a crime, communicate with deceased loved ones, or foretell the future. This sometimes involves inducing a trance state or the use of psychotropic products. Some healers who work on the spiritual level also include dream work and full spirit possession in their repertoire.

Like the curandero, the brujo must work in harmony with nature, remaining tuned in to the plants, stones, colors, animals, and other energies of the world. Special focus rests with the natural products indigenous to the area in which the brujo works. The products the land produces in a certain area are thought to have greater impact on the problems that manifest in that same area. When preparing an amulet or spell bag for a client, they must feel the virtues of the natural products they use to know how to best heal the circumstances.

A curandera uses herbs and tinctures, as well as prayer, rituals, and cleansing, to heal the afflicted, while a bruja approaches healing from primarily a magical perspective.

You will notice that these identifications strongly resemble the root doctor and the conjure doctor in Hoodoo and the granny doctor and goomer doctor in Granny Magic. In fact, just as with Granny Magic, Brujería and Curanderismo incorporate elements of Conjure from Hoodoo. If one considers the geographical layout of the southern United States, it is easy to see how the regions dominated by Brujería and Curanderismo interweave with Hoodoo areas, just as Granny Magic connects with Hoodoo from the northeast.

Granny doctors rarely left Appalachia and the Ozarks. Brujas and curanderas remained primarily in the southern and southwestern United States. Hoodoo, however, was on the move through the African diaspora, migrating north and west in the United States. Its influence, therefore, impressively informed each of the other folk magic systems.

——— 16 ———
History of
Brujería/Curanderismo

The Mexican-American magical paths are different from Granny Magic and Hoodoo in one very distinct way. The Scotch-Irish immigrated here of their own will and, as such, were forced to adapt their folk magic practices to a foreign environment. The Africans were kidnapped and relocated to America against their will and, as such, were forced to adapt their folk magic practices to a foreign environment.

In contrast, those we now call Mexican-Americans were always here and their practice continued uninterrupted for centuries in what would become the United States. Originally, Mexico included parts of modern-day Oregon, California, Arizona, Nevada, Utah, Texas, and as far east as Lousiana, as well as small parts of Colorado and Wyoming. Most of the southwestern United States was Mexico until

1848 when the Treaty of Guadalupe Hidalgo created the borders that we recognize today.

The changes brought about when this treaty was signed meant that people who had been Mexican before were now Americans. Other than the fact that slavery was illegal in Mexico and women were allowed to own land, which was not the case in the United States, life did not change much for the residents of those areas. They were still the people indigenous to the land who practiced the ancestral healing techniques, some of which originated in the ancient Aztec cultures.

Native Americans have lived in what is now California for more than 13,000–15,000 years, with an estimated population of around 300,000 at the time of the Spanish invasion of 1519. Archeological evidence indicates that Native American tribes lived in what is now New Mexico as far back as 9200 BC.

The Spanish conquest brought an influx of Mexican and Spanish immigrants to what is now California, Nevada, Utah, New Mexico, and Arizona. They co-mingled with the Native American populations there, sharing herbal and ritual healing practices that dated back to the Toltec empire of AD 387. The terrain, wildlife, and botanical environment of the western United States resembled that of Mexico, so the level of adaptation was far less extreme than that of the creators of Hoodoo or Granny Magic. The ancient practices transferred and blended almost seamlessly, creating an uninterrupted historical flow.

Mexico, including the parts of it that extended into the present-day United States, did not suffer political and religious demonization of magical practice until the Spanish invasion. Without the oppression of the Roman influence and its denigration of non-Christian supernatural practice, the cultural norm of Mexico embraced rituals, herb lore, advanced healing practices, and a copious amount of human sacrifice to keep the rain coming to nourish the grain crops.

In Mexico, the primary religious rites came from sun worshippers and rain worshippers, each of which demanded an impressive quantity of fresh human hearts and human blood. The rain cults equated the amount of human and animal blood that flowed to the amount of rain they would receive for their crops. Since they lived in a desert, rain was vital to their survival. They believed that if they stopped offering the sacrifices to feed the gods, the gods would die and take the rain with them.

The Goddess Coatlicue, for instance, is an earth goddess who created all celestial bodies: the moon, the stars, and the sun. She wears a necklace of human hearts and hands. Her body is made entirely of serpents. The Aztecs recognized her as a cannibalistic deity who was particularly fond of human hearts to eat and add to her fashion accessories.

In the film *Indiana Jones and the Temple of Doom*, we see an elaborate ritual to the Goddess Kali Ma, in which a priest removes the heart of a victim to offer to the goddess. Although Kali Ma is, in fact, a Hindu deity, she is equated with Coatlicue.

According to mythology, the Gods Quetzalcoatl and Tezcatlipoca ripped apart the Earth Goddess Cipactli, a reptilian dragon beast, to create the world using her body parts. To repay her for her sacrifice, the Aztecs consoled her with frequent offerings of human blood and hearts.

The Montezuma dynasty encouraged the practice of human sacrifice and used the offerings to leverage divine favor. They created unprecedented displays of architecture in the form of palaces, temples, and great canals, as well as extending the Aztec dominion ever beyond its boundaries.

By the time the Spanish conquered the Aztec Empire, there were too many people practicing these historical magical techniques for the conquistadors to effectively force conversion to Christianity, the religion of the conquerors.

Instead, the Spanish priests employed an "assimilate rather than eliminate" approach. Not all the Aztec gods demanded human sacrifice or blood offerings like the ones worshiped by the conquered regime. The Spanish priests brought attention back to the more benevolent Aztec gods and gradually equated them with the Catholic saints. This reprieve from ongoing human sacrifice demanded by the previous ruling paradigm was well-received by the masses, which allowed the syncretized blend to quickly spread throughout the country.

The people indigenous to Mexico had no conflict with the Catholic saints and quickly integrated them into their existing pantheon of holy figures. They understood that they could honor their gods just as well if they aligned them with similar Spanish holy figures. The veneration of the Blessed Mother in the form of the Virgin Mary took hold, and to this day, Our Lady of Guadalupe, the most common presentation of the

Virgin Mary in Mexico, remains its most celebrated and popular holy figure.

Thinking they were invading a barbaric and primitive culture, the Spanish conquistadors were surprised to find a sophisticated and systematic socialized health-care system, complete with hospitals manned by healers armed with an advanced knowledge of herbal healing and an impressive body of medicinal research. Although many of the hospitals were destroyed in the conquest, the medical networks remained intact and continue through to the present time.

Expanding this herbal and ritual-based health care system, the Spaniards added Judeo-Christian scriptures as magical incantations, as well as the use of the crucifix and images of saints as magical talismans. Numbers routinely used for magical rituals—such as how many times to perform a spell or how long to keep a ritual going—are 3, 7, 9, 11, and 13, all of which are Judeo-Christian magical numerical concepts.

The Spanish introduced the Greek humoral medical perspectives to Curanderismo, as well as Arabic medicinal practices from the Moors and elements of medieval and post-medieval European Witchcraft. In fact, the Spanish priests and healers who came to Mexico during and after the conquest found that many of their magico-religious beliefs resembled those of the Aztec people. This compatibility of practice further assisted the assimilation of the two cultures.

European Witchcraft interjected the concept of humans controlling supernatural forces, rather than the other way around. The Hispanic-Arabic system of healing brought the wisdom of treating the mind, body, and spirit with harmonic balance and connecting the process of healing to the existing environment in a holistic fashion. These two factors were influential in solidifying what would become the long-term perspectives of both Brujería and Curanderismo.

In addition to the numbers used, the Judeo-Christian concept that humans can heal in the name of God just as Christ instructed his disciples to do, became a primary aspect of Curanderismo. Curanderos tap into supernatural power—meaning God in their theology—through prayer, visualization, incantations, and ritual, then use the synergistic power created by that engagement to heal.

From an occultist perspective of the practice, both the brujas and the curanderas see, influence, and communicate with supernatural beings such as spirits and angels. This is one of the many historical and modern distinctions between the bruja and the curandera. The bruja supposedly accesses her supernatural power through the Christian devil and the curandera from the Christian god. The curandero heals, while the brujo harms. Malevolent spirits create discord and benevolent spirits bless. This duality of light and dark between the two roles is persistent and greatly informs overall public opinion, when again, the practices are almost identical when we strip away the kneejerk societal biases.

This multiculturally influenced healing system migrated over centuries into what would become the western and southwestern United States, and blended with the practices of Native Americans local to the area, ultimately creating the Brujería and Curanderismo of the United States today.

Unfortunately, the lack of pre-conquest documentation muddies the perception of which current practices came from which culture, so what is left is informed speculation. Additionally, from a philosophical perspective, most of the primary influences in Mexican magic and healing were remarkably akin to one another. This overlapping and cooperative integration allowed for a mutually-informative blend of practices, but creates a challenge in fully identifying the distinct contribution of each culture.

Even after the Louisiana Purchase redefined the boundaries of the United States, in many areas of the Southwest, larger towns in Mexico were geographically closer than larger towns in the United States. This led Mexican people living in the United States to seek out medical care from the curanderas of Mexico, not only because it was their familiar and societal norm, but also because they were the nearest medical assistance. In the vast, sparsely populated spaces between towns during the 1800–1900s, the curandera was often the only option for medical care. As insurance and immigration considerations took hold, health care became even more restricted, especially for undocumented people of Mexican heritage in the United States.

Now, as they did throughout the past, curanderos and brujos serve the rural poor, addressing both the spiritual and physical aspects of healing. In each path, the training is academic and experiential, drawing on the vast body of herbal healing lore from the Aztec and Mayan healers, with North American Native American influences, as well as the many cross-cultural components brought to Mexico by the Spanish.

Curanderismo is nothing if not adaptable, and from its prehistoric origins to its modern presentation, it demonstrates an eagerness to soak up new information. Contemporary curanderas welcome scientific medical knowledge and use it alongside their traditional healing practices. The curandera works effectively with scientific-based medicine, and although the Westernized medical industry may criticize the curandero for giving equal significance to the psychological, social, and spiritual aspects of healing, the curandera ridicules Westernized medicine for its lack of attention to this vital part of the curative process.

The history of Curanderismo and its darker sibling, Brujería, is as old as Mexico itself and parallels the cultural, religious, and historical progress of Mexican-Americans into the current time. Each of the earliest Mexican immigrants who moved north into the wilds of what is now the southwestern and western United States brought a part of Curanderismo and Brujería with them. Now those practices flourish in any part of the United States where Mexican-American communities exist. You may not see it, especially if you are not in the culture, but it is there. It is always there.

—————— 17 ——————
Basic Beliefs of Brujería/Curanderismo

Brujería and Curanderismo differ from Granny Magic and Hoodoo in that the teaching and apprenticeship processes are less centered on hierarchy. Although there is a designated teacher, the mindset is that the teacher will learn from the student as well as the student learning from the teacher, which levels the playing field in the relationship in everything but experience level.

Brujería and Curanderismo are not limited by boundaries of cultural, racial, or ancestral entitlement. One is born a bruja or curandera or they are not, regardless of their ethnicity, religion, or lineage. If a person identifies as a curandera or bruja and demonstrates an aptitude for magic and healing, they are welcomed into and warmly accepted by the Hispanic magical community. The concept of a "calling" or being born with the compulsion to heal and work magic for others is a time-honored practice within the culture. This is exclusive of any other identifying markers such as race, culture, or social class.

For many who are called to study Brujería or Curanderismo, there is a sense of "coming home," as though they always knew this was what they were meant to do and they relate to the lifestyle and techniques in a way that is almost supernatural. There is a feeling of fitting in and rightness that permeates the learning and adapting process when a person feels they are meant to be in the practice. This is the energy that the brotherhood and sisterhood of Brujería and Curanderismo honor.

This stark difference from the territorialism of the Hoodoo world was a blessing for which I was personally ill-prepared. When I first received my calling as a bruja, I was concerned that the Hispanic and Latino community would reject me outright for being basically the whitest person on earth. My fears were ill-founded, and once I set up shop and began my practice, they embraced me as a sister, a mother, and a friend. In the years I have practiced as a bruja, never once have I felt maligned, marginalized, belittled, disrespected, or unwelcome in the Hispanic/Latino community. They even tolerate my limited pidgin Spanish and work hard to communicate effectively with me.

When I began my public practice, members of the Hispanic community around my shop stepped up to help, advising me in the subtle, unwritten traditions of practice that are impossible to find anywhere unless you just *know*. For instance, it was my inclination as a business owner to quietly advertise my presence in other local businesses that catered to the Hispanic community. One of my advisors, with a panicked expression, warned me I should *never* do so, because, culturally, it is the act of the novice or charlatan to advertise. He assured me that knowledge of my presence and the quality of my work would spread by word of mouth and, in fact, already had.

"Just be patient, *mi amiga*," he insisted. "Be patient and it will happen." He was correct and saved me from a major cultural faux pas.

A few months into my active practice, an elderly woman came into the shop to update me on the positive results of a limpia (ritual cleansing) I performed on her grandson. As she excitedly told me of his progress, she said, "We are so glad you are here." I was surprised by this high praise coming from an elder in the community and shared with her my concerns of the community feeling I was appropriating their culture. Her eyes got big and she said, "Oh no! We LOVE our Gringa Bruja." That made me laugh and is how I acquired my working name, "Gringa Bruja."

Within five hundred feet of my shop, there was a second botánica run by a woman who *is* fully Latina. Our relationship was warm and cooperative, and we frequently sent customers to and from one another. I am forever grateful that this loving culture welcomed their Gringa Bruja with open arms. I have found this attitude to be prevalent within the Hispanic magical community and not just in my own geographical area. Since my calling and subsequent immersion into the practice several years ago, I have seen no discrimination or rejection of non-Hispanic or non-Christian people who are called to practice the art. If you are called and enter the process with good intent, you are welcomed.

Brujería and Curanderismo are apprenticed paths, and most of the time when a person receives the call to work as a bruja or curandero, the teacher appears. Both teacher and student are well tuned to know when the student is ready to work independently, and a synchronized and simpatico understanding flows between them, provided the student-teacher dynamic is solid. One of the first things one learns in the study of Brujería is that there is no room for ego. One must place oneself aside in deference to the needs of the client and the demands of the spirit world. This mindset also influences the teacher-student relationship, in which ego of being the educated and experienced teacher is less important than the shared learning experience between the two.

Brujería is defined as the living, continual magical and spiritual path of Mesoamerica (Mexico) that dates to the beginning of Aztec civilization. It is an oral tradition passed on from teacher to apprentice, and to this day, very little instruction is available in written form. Mary Devine wrote a book called *The Magic of Mexico* that is one of the few books available in English on the subject. Most of my own study came from books translated out of Spanish by my husband and relayed to me verbally. Even in the Spanish language, few books exist outlining the details of the practice.

Channeling supernatural entities, those that once lived as humans and those that were never incarnate, is a key component to both Brujería and Curanderismo. A common practice is to channel gifted healers who have passed on into death. El Niño Fidencio and Aurorita are two of these healers who often appear to curanderas to summon them into practice or who are deliberately sought out in spirit form to direct their talents to the working curandera.

Both Fidencio and Aurorita have cult-like groups of worshippers who work exclusively with those ancestral energies. Followers of Fidencio are called "Fidencistas." They are exclusively vegetarians with tremendous reverence for flowers and other plant life. Their ambition is to cultivate happiness and spiritualism throughout the world.

Niño Fidencio was a nineteenth-century healer who performed surgery without tools or anesthesia, reportedly with no pain to the patient. He performed many miracles, such as healing lame patients so they could walk and blind patients so they could see.

Aurorita was a child healer who died in a house fire at the age of six. In the nineteenth century, she performed many miracles of record in Monterrey, Mexico, and is a potent healing spirit.

Teresa Urrea, also referenced as "Teresita" or "Santa Teresa of Cabora" is a famous nineteenth-century curandera who received divine healing abilities and visions from the Virgin Mary following a serious illness. Ultimately, thousands of people sought her out for healing and blessings.

Although the Catholic church does not reference any of these healers as officially canonized saints, they are venerated as folk saints in the Mexican culture.

Martyrdom is a strong component of Curanderismo, and many curanderas see literally hundreds of patients in a single day. Some healers die from the symptoms of exhaustion. Within the Latin and Hispanic communities, a strong religious significance lies in the concept of suffering to gain. Specifically, the imitation of the suffering of Christ or of the saints is a common theme.

Pilgrimages are a frequent component, often with the penitents crawling on their knees or rolling on their sides (like a logroll) to the shrine or other target of the pilgrimage. Holy statues are decorated and processed through crowds, held aloft and venerated as part of these sacred journeys. Pilgrims ritualistically ingest dirt from the area of the shrine, either on its own or in tonics, to carry the blessings of the holy place within their bodies for healing or spiritual sanctity.

While some of the practices of the curanderos, devotees, and brujos may, like those of rootworkers and granny doctors, seem foreign or primitive to the viewpoint of modern society, the experience is something one truly must live to understand. To judge the presented spiritual expression without feeling firsthand the energy of the veneration profoundly minimizes the impact and emotion of the experience. One can say the same about nearly any spiritual or religious rites and observations. There is a spirit that flows through such venerations that defies explanation or description.

Mexican American healers give the same consideration to the physical and mundane causes for illness as they do to the supernatural causes. If the client's problem is of a supernatural cause and is merely manifesting as physical symptoms, treating only the physical symptoms will not cure the root problem. Many curanderas and brujas believe that the root cause of most mental illnesses is the failure to address a spiritual problem manifesting as a physical problem. Such a condition might be caused either by an attack, such as *mal de ojo* (the evil eye) or the development of some spiritual upheaval deriving from guilt, jealousy, depression, or frustration.

Dis-ease, in this set of cultural beliefs, is caused by disharmony, within the spirit, the mind, the body, or some imbalance in the essential communication between the three. That disharmony might be something as simple as germ theory: the patient became ill from exposure to a virus or some type of bacteria. There may also be a shadow aspect of the disease that comes from a spiritual or mental disturbance and manifests in physical form. This spiritual aspect of illness, its shadow side, is their explanation for why illnesses often strike one person in a family and not everyone. An illness of physical cause is random, but an illness of spiritual cause is deeply personal.

The healer must also evaluate the patient from a socioeconomic and environmental perspective. Illness has a different effect on a person who provides for a large family than it does for a child who is dependent on his or her parents. For this reason, all aspects—physical, spiritual, psychological, environmental, and social—hold essential clues to the cause of symptoms, which in turn inform the most effective treatment and cure for the condition.

Curanderas and brujas believe that no illness caused by magical means is incurable. It must, however, first be discovered and named to be cured. The standard thought is, "What can be done to a person can be undone."

Brujería and Curanderismo work far more cooperatively with modern medicine than modern medicine works with them. The brujo and curandero's biggest complaint and concern about the mainstream medical approach is its limited view that a patient's physical symptoms should only be evaluated and treated on a physical level. Mainstream caregivers typically do not investigate other levels of care unless and until all physical causes are ruled out. If the cause is found to be "psychosomatic," the caregiver treats the patient as though they are at fault for their illness or tells them dismissively that the condition is "all in their head." This is the exact opposite of the Curanderismo approach.

Curanderas and brujas view magic not as subjective or imaginary, but as empirical. It is observable, with results that are tested, trackable, evolving, duplicable, and just as reliable as any used in scientific healing. Science says, "If you apply healing practices A, B, and C, in that order, to condition X, you will usually, but not always, see result Y." Magical healing espouses the exact same premise, but on a supernatural level. The bruja and curandera feels there is no more reason to doubt the efficacy of certain herbs, rituals, and incantations as there is to doubt that aspirin, rest, and fluids will reliably cure a headache. Just as medicinal cures are variable, often needing several different pharmaceutical and therapeutic approaches before finding the right treatment, so is magical healing variable.

In modern medicine, if a cure does not work, the treatment—or worse, the patient or condition—is blamed, rather than the caregiver. In Brujería and Curanderismo, the fault lies not with the cure or the magic, but with the healer. If they are unable to cure a person of a condition that affects their quality of life, it is because the healer did not explore all avenues of causation and determine the correct treatment.

Of the healing modalities employed by the curandero or brujo, the most common are the *plática,* the *limpia,* and the *barrida.*

A plática is an in-depth, nonjudgmental therapy session a bruja or a curandera has with a client, not only as part of the evaluation process, but also as an essential component of the healing process. During the plática, the client unburdens themselves to the healer, sharing their experiences that led them to their current dilemma, expressing accountability or denial of culpability for their actions, and identifying their goals and hopes for the future. If a client is not forthcoming, the healer might use alternative therapies, such as art or light hypnosis, to assist. The client is sometimes asked to present their dreams for analysis during this time. The plática creates an arena for trust between the healer and the clients so that further work may be done without inhibitions or boundaries.

Part interview and part unburdening session, the plática is an important part of the healing process for both the healer and the client.

A limpia is an intense, ritualized, comprehensive cleansing of the mind, body, and spirit. The classic limpia involves cleansing with the smoke of burning herbs, the rolling of eggs, limes, or lemons on the body, and magical sprays and oils.

A barrida is like the limpia, but also incorporates a ritualized sweeping of the body using an actual broom or a bundle of specialized herbs. During the barrida or limpia, the healer tunes into the client completely, opening to any messages the body or divine forces send. Eggs, lemons, or limes are sometimes rolled over the client's body with an emphasis on the lymphatic areas and any part of the body that the healer registers as contaminated.

The eggs, lemons, or limes absorb the negative energy from the body. As the healer rolls them over the body, he or she recites an incantation such as the Lord's Prayer or the Apostle's Creed. Traditionally, both the client and the healer remove all rings and any metal from their bodies during this process, as the metal can interrupt the flow of healing energy or redirect the energy from its intended target area. The healer also uses copious amounts of white sage smoke or palo santo smoke to assist with the cleansing, as well as various natural sprays and oils.

Following a detailed consultation, the limpia or barrida is traditionally the first step in healing. In most cases, with careful, concerted attention from the healer, this treatment is all that is needed to create balance and start the repair process in the body and spirit.

Invested as they are in the natural expressions of the Divine for healing, curanderos and brujos alike incorporate the four elements of earth, air, fire, and water into their practices. Fire provides direct communication with the supernatural forces and acts as an intermediary between humans and energies beyond the physical realm. Fire is used not only for scrying in coals, but as part of the purification process during a limpia or barrida.

Using a candle, the healer can trace *crucitas,* or "little crosses," over the body of the person being cleansed, with attention paid to dark areas or parts of the body that feel energetically congested or off balance. The candle and heat never touch the patient, but are used to conduct healing energy to the afflicted areas.

Holy water provides a physical link to the spirit world and is used to anoint and bless people and tools. Oils and incenses (earth and air) please the spirit world and attract benevolent spirits to help with the healing process.

Although animal sacrifice is still occasionally used, many brujas and curanderas use an egg instead. The egg, representative of an animal cell, acts as an acceptable substitute for a live animal sacrifice. Eggs are especially effective in cases of *mal de ojo* (the evil eye). After cleansing, the egg is cracked into a jar, read as an oracle, and safely discarded. In my own practice, after using an egg to purify a client, I have seen the egg break to reveal contents that are black, red like blood, or putrefied, even though it was a known good egg at the start of the procedure.

A brujo or curandero may also be tasked with the job of cleaning a home, called "incensing" or just cleansing. This process is like Native American smudging and involves a systematic purging of all areas of the home using smoke (from burning sage or palo santo), holy water, specially created washes, and sometimes stones or crystals. Clients often seek this type of home healing after a death in the family, a divorce, during times of strife, or if they feel they have been crossed (cursed) by someone else.

In addition to these techniques, a curandero may utilize therapeutic massage and, in fact, employ what is now called "reflexology," healing through acupressure applied to certain reactive areas on the soles of the feet and hands. In Mexico, this method of healing was used before any written history currently available and remains a vital component of Curanderismo. The specific liniments and ointments for the procedure are also sympathetic to the condition and lend herbal medicinal assistance.

Brewed teas using flowers, herbs, and roots are a primary component of the healing process, as are tinctures, concoctions, decoctions, salves, and oils. Valerian (*valeriana*), rue (*ruta*), chamomile (called *manzanilla*), borage (*borraja*), garlic (*ajo*), rosemary (*romero*), cannabis, orange blossoms, salvias, and other healing herbs are essential to the curandera and the bruja, often using recipes that date back into pre-history.

The curanderas believe that every person, animal, and object emits its own *"vibraciones"* (vibrations), which are in constant flux as the person, animal, or object absorbs vibraciones from the influences in the environment. This creates a steady flow of energy between all things and, most importantly, creates a mutable field in which the healer can work. The energy influences may be positive or negative, depending on the variables and the baseline energy inherent to the person, animal, or object. The energies of animals and objects, such as stones and crystals, can shift the energy of people and assist with the healing process. The material objects, such as stones of certain vibratory levels, can alter the body forces that cause illness or misfortune and commute them to heal instead of harm.

Many curanderos and brujos depend on trancework to take them between the worlds for communion with the spirits and the ancestors, as well as to channel the wisdom of healers who have passed on to death. In a shamanistic fashion, the curandera and bruja use a combination of trance and channeling to diagnose, prognosticate, and cure, as well as to manipulate various spiritual currents both in the body and outside of the patient.

Through these trances, the healer can often tell if someone has cursed or crossed the patient. Usually, if this is identified as the problem, the impression is that a brujo or bruja did so on the behalf of an enemy of the victim. In some practices, this means healing the victim by punishing the perpetrator. When the healer transmutes the energy of the curse to return it to the one who sent it, the patient's symptoms often resolve. This type of work causes a curandero to walk a fine line that is very close to Brujería in purposefully inflicting damage onto a person through supernatural means.

If a client is cursed, one of the first things they want to know is the identity of the person who cursed them. Some brujos and curanderos, including myself, refuse to disclose the information, believing that the victim will not continue the healing process if they engage in retaliatory actions. The preferred response is to allow the energy to return to the sender and free the patient to heal properly.

A deliberate magical attack sent by another person may result in symptoms that are physical (manifesting as hives, boils, a wasting illness, or other condition), social (such as bad luck, car problems, marital conflict, difficult children, employment problems, or other forms of prolonged, serial misfortunes), or psychological (including nightmares, panic attacks, depression, paranoia, or other forms of mental breakdown or detriment).

In any of these signs of magical attack, cursing, or crossing, the curandero manages and treats the physical ailment, helps to resolve the social dysfunctions, offers treatment to reduce or resolve the psychological problems, provides magical work to relieve ongoing misfortune, and changes both the patient's outlook and their prospects for the better. This is in addition to reversing the energy flow that caused the problems in the first place.

Common conditions of the mind, body, and spirit that a curandero might be asked to cure are:

Susto: A condition of spiritual or magical fright, very much like post-traumatic stress syndrome, resulting in symptoms resembling a panic attack, depression, and an inability to successfully resume normal life after a trauma. Treatment is a specific ritual involving a white sheet, a broom, and a limpia or barrida, accompanied by the recitation of the Apostle's Creed. Ideally, treatment begins immediately after the trauma, preferably before the patient sleeps again.

Bilis: A condition of suppressed, *inwardly* directed anger and fear resulting in the creation of bile within the body. This causes gastrointestinal disorders, generalized anxiety, headaches, and appetite dysfunction. A bilis is treated with laxatives and purgatives in conjunction with a full limpia.

Muina: A condition of *outwardly* directed anger resulting in episodes of rage and violence that may cumulatively result in symptoms of physical ailment such as paralysis, loss of appetite, flushing, swelling of body parts, or physical deformities such as hunchback or a drawn arm. Anger is thought to poison the body over time and in the case of muina, the only way to discharge the rage is through a full limpia, repeated three or nine times, depending on the severity of the condition.

Empacho: A blockage in the intestines or stomach, usually caused by an undigested bolus of food. Symptoms include indigestion, vomiting, lack of appetite, diarrhea, or constipation. The condition is treated with emetics, laxatives, and a full limpia. A client might suffer an empacho from things left unsaid that should be said or from unrequited or imbalanced love in relationships.

Mal aire: A condition caused by chilly or nighttime air entering the body by breathing or through the skin. It manifests with flu-like symptoms, earache, or muscle soreness. Translating literally to "bad air," mal aire is a supernatural cause of illness rather than a physical one and is thought to be caused by bad spirits in the air. Treatment is a full limpia and herbal cleansing tonics.

Mal de ojo: A condition resulting from a person, particularly an attractive or talented child, being admired or envied by someone else, without touching the object of their admiration or envy, to discharge the feeling. Touching the person/child in effect humanizes them and releases the envy felt by the other person. Without the touch, the object of the admiration may fall ill, requiring a specific type of cleansing to remove the evil eye. Treatment is an aggressive limpia and egg cleansing. Mal de ojo is common in young babies, resulting from the "What a *cute baby!*" forms of admiration. Fortunately, babies *love* egg cleansings and usually coo all the way through it and then take a long nap afterward.

These are examples of healing on a material level. To heal the above conditions, as well as actual physical ailments, injuries, or the results of a magical attack, the bruja or curandera uses common everyday items combined with traditional rituals, as described. They may ask for the intervention of and use images of various Catholic saints known to provide sympathetic healing to the condition causing the patient to seek out help. The healer must set up careful protection for the patient as the healing process takes place. While the client is undergoing treatment, their spirit is in flux and is thereby vulnerable to possession by evil entities.

Cooking and the use of foods to heal, particularly through cold and hot foods meant to address the temperatures of the humors in the body, may also be used to heal and administer certain herbal remedies. Religious symbols, candles, ribbons and cords, holy water and washes, incenses, teas, baths, and amulets are all part of the healing arsenal of the curandero and brujo.

Divination

Divination is a primary component to both Brujería and Curanderismo. Either of these practitioners may use forms of divination such as tarot cards, a standard poker deck, or the forty-card Mexican deck to obtain additional information about their patient, the condition, or the symptoms that caused the patient to seek help.

The level of smoke from the burning sage used during a limpia or a barrida is another form of divination often used, as is bibliomancy. Bibliomancy is the use of books in divination, usually a holy book such as the Bible. The healer anoints themselves, usually on the temples and palms, with an oil conducive to prophecy or psychic awareness. They connect with spirit or ancestral guides to assist them and close their eyes while holding the book and focusing on their question. Without opening their eyes, they run their hands over the closed book, over the cover, the spine, and the closed pages. They then gently move their fingers over the pages until they feel a tug or a draw to a certain location in the book. Still without looking, they open the book to that area and place their hands on the pages. They then run their hands over the pages until the find the passage that pulls their fingers to it. They put their finger on that passage, then open their eyes to read the selected words, which contain a message for them relating to the question they asked.

Another type of divination involves reading the ashes of a cigar or cigarette smoked by the healer, noting how the ash curls and what shape it takes when it drops away. This is similar to tea leaf reading.

A Tale of Two Sisters

The two primary holy figures of Mexican spirituality, both in Mexico and in the United States, are female. Although they are not at all related through either theology or mythology, their very polarity draws them into a light and dark contrast that is reflective of the dichotomy of Curanderismo and Brujería. The most venerated saint in this culture is Our Lady of

Guadalupe, a cultural interpretation of the Virgin Mary, the Blessed Mother of Jesus Christ.

The Catholic Church aggressively demonizes the second most popular saint, refusing to acknowledge her as any kind of spiritual entity. Still, she remains not only a popular folk saint, but the focus of many cults and temples. Her name is Santa Muerte (Holy Death) or La Santisima Muerte (The Holiest Death).

While Our Lady of Guadalupe is the epitome of light, Santa Muerte is the Queen of Darkness. Guadalupe is pious and pure, while Santa Muerte is a party girl. Each saint commands her own devoted, extensive following.

Our Lady of Guadalupe

The story of Our Lady of Guadalupe is a beautiful mixture of mythology and mystery. The most objective studies show her roots in the Mexican moon Goddess *Tonantzin (*Our Revered Mother), then later syncretized to the Virgin Mary after the Spanish conquest. She is the official patron saint of Mexico and is also known as the Queen of Mexico. Where crucifixes dominate the Catholic churches of the United States, in Mexico you will instead find representations of Our Lady of Guadalupe.

On December 9, 1531, a man named Juan Diego Cuauhtlatoatzin was walking in the Tepayac hills near Mexico City on his way to a Franciscan mission to receive religious instruction. Some legends identify him as a peasant, while others say he was a wealthy and influential man. A woman appeared to him and identified herself as the Holy Mother of Jesus. She requested a shrine erected in her honor at that location so that she could help the poor and afflicted who would make pilgrimages to it.

As requested, Juan Diego delivered the message to the acting bishop, Fray Juan Zumárraga, who told him that he needed to pray about the request and that he should return the next day. Disappointed by the lack of follow-through or interest on the part of the bishop, Juan Diego returned to the same location and the woman appeared to him again. He told her about his failure and suggested she find someone of greater worth and influence to act on her behalf.

She insisted that he was the one to undertake the task and asked him to return to the bishop and repeat her request. The next day, after a period of prayer and contemplation, the bishop was more amenable to the request, but insisted on a sign to prove the vision was authentic.

Juan Diego returned to the site later that day and the Virgin again appeared, telling him to come back the following day for his proof. Unfortunately, Juan Diego's uncle fell gravely ill and he was tasked to go find a priest to hear his uncle's deathbed confession and administer last rites. Juan Diego knew this task would prevent him from returning as the woman ordered, so he took a different route into town hoping to avoid her. She intercepted him anyway, asking him what he was doing and why he was avoiding her. When he explained his dilemma, she replied saying, "*No estoy yo aqui que soy tu madre?*" ("Am I not here, I who am your mother?")

She assured him that his uncle was already recovered and instructed him to climb a nearby hill and collect the flowers growing there. He did as she said and was surprised to find a field of flowers growing where there had previously been only cacti and scrub. With his cloak, called a *tilma*, still tied around his neck, he gathered the flowers into its folds and returned to her. She rearranged the flowers and told him to take them to the bishop.

He did so the same day, and when he opened his cloak in front of the bishop and other holy men assembled in the room, the flowers fell out onto the floor, revealing an image of the Virgin Mary stained onto the tilma, presumably by the flowers.

Juan Diego returned home to find his uncle not only recovered, but telling his own story of seeing a vision of the Mother of Christ who instructed him to tell the bishop of his miracle healing and that she now wished to be called "Guadalupe."

Now fully convinced, the bishop got to work and on December 26, 1531, Our Lady of Guadalupe had her first shrine constructed on the site where she appeared. It was a hastily-built monument that would change over the years. From that day forward, the tilma worn by Juan Diego has been displayed at the shrine, which is now a great basilica visited by more than twenty million pilgrims each year. Inscribed over the main entrance of the basilica are the words Guadalupe said to Juan Diego: *"No estoy yo aqui que soy tu madre?"* Juan

Diego himself was canonized as Saint Juan Diego Cuauhtlatoatzin in 2002.

All that sounds like so much fanciful fairy tale and para-
ble; however, the tilma Juan Deigo wore is itself a supernatural phenomenon that continues to defy scientific explanation.

It is made of the poor quality, rough surface, cactus-based
material that was common to cloaks of the 1500s. The image
of Guadalupe, on the other hand, is said to be "like silk."
The image is not just a blotchy, ink blot-type rendering that
may or may not be a female form if you squint and look at it
sideways. This is no "Christ's image in a piece of burnt toast"
grade of a miracle. The image is a very elaborate, intricate figure with meticulous detail, reminiscent of the Italian frescos.
The colors are iridescent and shift hue depending on where
you stand as you view it.

Infrared examination shows no brush strokes or undersketching to indicate it is a painting. The creation of such a detailed artistic work without the use of any undersketching in
a pre-digital art era is basically impossible and scientists quite
literally cannot explain how it was made. A biophysicist from
Florida, Phillip Callahan, conducted an extensive study of the
tilma and his analysis is, "Such a technique would be an impossible accomplishment in human hands" (Sennott, 53).

The image has no animal or mineral elements known to
humans and synthetic colors did not exist in 1531. From the
time it came into Fray Juan Zumárraga's hands on December 12, 1531 when Juan Diego untied it from around his own

neck until the present time, there is no known compromise to the line of custody of the tilma.

Artists attempted to authentically replicate the tilma many times, but the original consistently outlives the duplicates. The best copy remained under glass, displayed next to the original, and disintegrated in only eight years' time. In contrast, the original was displayed fully exposed to air for over one hundred and sixteen years and is now over four hundred and seventy-five years old. The natural life of a cloak of this material from that time is approximately thirty years. The tilma also maintains a constant temperature of 98.6 degrees Fahrenheit.

A Peruvian ophthalmologist magnified the image by 2,500 times and determined that within the eyes, there are as many as thirteen different human figures depicted. According to legend, there were thirteen people in the room when Juan Diego opened his tilma for the Bishop.

In 1709, a worker was cleaning the glass over the tilma and accidentally spilled a strong nitric acid cleaning solvent onto a large portion of the tilma. The acid should have immediately eaten away the image, but the image restored itself over the next thirty days and today is unscathed. Stains from the accident are evident in the areas of the tilma that do not have the image.

In 1921, an activist hid a bomb containing twenty-nine sticks of dynamite in a pot of roses and placed it before the tilma. The bomb exploded, shattering 150 feet of windows behind the tilma and twisting a nearby marble altar rail and a brass crucifix out of shape. The tilma and its protective glass were unharmed.

Astrologers studied the configuration of stars on the robe of the figure in the image and determined that they are arranged in exact replication of the constellations in the sky on December 12, 1531.

It is unknown why the figure in the tilma's image is clearly Indian or Hispanic in appearance when the Virgin Mary, according to the Bible, was Jewish.

Each year on December 12, the date of her first appearance to Don Juan, approximately six million people participate in the annual pilgrimage to view the tilma and pray to Our Lady of Guadalupe. Her basilica in Mexico is the most visited Catholic shrine in the world.

La Santisima Muerte

She is known as *La Niña Blanca* (the white girl), *La Flaquita* (the skinny girl), *La Dama Poderosa* (the powerful woman), *La Huesuda* (the bony lady), and *Santísima Muerte* (most holy saint of death), but originally, she was *Mictecacihuatl* (Lady of the land of the dead). Her followers speak of her with reverence and a smile, while others cross themselves and revile her.

She, above all others, is my *patrona*...my own patron saint.

The first day of every month, between two and four thousand devotees of La Santisima Muerte visit a shrine to her, located at a modest home in Tepito, Mexico. They bring her offerings, pray to her, touch the glass that separates them from her image, and hold hands to link contact between her shrine and those who cannot get close enough to experience her.

The home belongs to Doña Queta, also known as Enriqueta Romero, who in 2001, on a whim, erected a shrine to the folk saint in her front window, including a human-sized statue of Santa Muerte. What happened next was unprecedented. Devotees took notice and came out of the woodwork, flocking to the home to pay homage the honored saint of death.

Actual tracking of this saint's veneration is unclear, because until the shrine went up in Tepito, there was no public admission of her worship. Doña Queta is a typical devotee and says she has prayed to Santa Muerte since she was twelve years old. She is now in her seventies. This sort of underground following is common to Santa Muerte and makes it impossible to determine how long she has been the focus of such reverence.

She is one of the few saints with no human counterpart. She never lived and is based on no living person. She is the Grim Reaper. Tomás Prower, author of *La Santa Muerte: Unearthing the Magic & Mysticism of Death,* points out that when we see the Grim Reaper, all we ever see are bones and a hooded cloak. There is no gender distinction in the skeletal form, and yet the automatic assumption is that the Grim Reaper is male.

This is thought to come from the association of males as destroyers and takers of lives on the battlefield and when hunting. A competing thought, however, is that if females are the givers of life, then they might also be the ones who usher us out of the life they gave to us. In short, the Grim Reaper could just as easily be female as male.

Santa Muerte is not to be confused with Catrina, the famous sugar skull drawing made famous by artist Jose Guadalupe Posada during the Mexican Revolution to celebrate Dia de los Muertos. Catrina is also a skeletal form, but she was drawn as a political commentary to mock the second wife of Porfirio Diaz who served as the President of Mexico for thirty-one years and was criticized for living lavishly while his constituents starved. Catrina is invariably dressed as a socialite in fabulous style.

Images such as Catrina, used to celebrate Dia de los Muertos (Day of the Dead) and honor the beloved dead, are unaffiliated with Santa Muerte. She is also sometimes erroneously equated with the Santerían Orisha Oya, who serves as the guardian of the cemetery gates. Oya *is* the cemetery; Santa Muerte is death itself.

Since 2005, it has been illegal in Mexico, although not in the United States, to start a church with any version of "Santa Muerte" in the name. In March of 2009, a Mexican army destroyed more than forty shrines to Santa Muerte along the Mexico-United States border. The Catholic Church refuses to acknowledge Santa Muerte as an official saint and, in fact, is the force behind much of the propaganda to denigrate and malign her.

Ironically, the reason for all this national hostility toward Santa Muerte is her own benevolence. She is devoid of judgment toward any form of human behavior and is consequently associated with criminals, drug cartels, prostitutes, and the undesirable fringe elements of society. To her, anything we do as humans is simply an expression of humans being human. Nothing we do can ever compare to what she will do to us when she closes our eyes for the final time, and therefore, anything we do pales in comparison and is irrelevant. She has no concept of good or evil. She serves humankind as a powerful and intense force, as does death itself.

Her boredom and indifference with what we think of as degenerate or criminal behavior draws in the marginalized, the unrepentant, and those seeking power over others. In a pivotal scene in the AMC television show *Breaking Bad*, the Cousins, representatives of and hitmen from a Mexican drug cartel, join a pilgrimage to Santa Muerte, crawling on the ground in expensive suits and fancy boots, to one of her shrines. They then pin a photograph of "Heisenberg," the show's anti-hero, onto her robes as a request that she eliminate their enemy. For many Americans watching this popular show, this was their first and possibly only exposure to Santa Muerte.

She has a strong LGBTQ following, due to her accepting nature and total lack of discrimination. She demands no sacrifice, but works better if one is given. Common offerings are the items she enjoys: candy, marijuana joints, hard liquor (especially tequila) in tiny, airline bottles or shot glasses, money, games, chocolate, tobacco, or flowers. Rituals to honor her range from the simple lighting of a candle with *jaculatoria* (short prayers) to *novenas* (nine-day ritual prayers).

Her followers often clothe a skeleton to represent her, dressing her as a nun, a bride, a virgin, or a queen. She is also often portrayed wearing a multi-colored gown representing the seven chakra colors. But no matter her clothing, she is herself always in skeletal form.

The color of the robes Santa Muerte wears reflect the specialized work she embodies in that form. When her robes are green, her attention turns to money and matters of law. In black robes, she works for people who are denied justice or need protection from enemies. In red, she offers love and protection. Her white or ivory colored robes mean she provides harmony in the home and peace with one's neighbors. Blue robes denote the influence on mental powers, for academia and increased acuity. If she wears amber robes, she helps to fight addiction and dependency. If she is in purple robes, her focus is on healing of all kinds. In some cases, she is clothed in a rainbow-colored robe to cover all of these needs.

The power over *all* life—not just human life—is in her hands, so devotees also petition her to heal their pets or control the pests around them. People go to her to seek protection of all kinds, because who can better protect you from death than death herself? She both gives protection from death and brings death.

Her popularity eclipses all saints except for Guadalupe, and she has approximately five million admitted devotees in

Mexico (which amounts to 5 percent of the country's population) and approximately ten million followers worldwide. Temples to her are scattered throughout the Southwest; however, in most cases, you must know someone who knows someone to gain admittance. The theologies and practices surrounding her worship shift from temple to temple, and what one group believes about her often differs wildly from what the next group believes. She presents in many forms, and each interaction with her is highly personal and unique.

The owl is sacred to her, as are the crystal ball, the scythe, skulls, and the scales; any configuration of these items may appear by her side.

Previously, in my own shop, the shrine to Santa Muerte was a frequent focus for visitors. Some would come into the shop, give her an offering and pray to her, then leave with only a nod but not a word to us. We knew that this was the reason the shrine was there and we never took offense. The visitors were not there for us, but for her. Others would cross themselves and leave as soon as they saw her in her shelf below the fixed candles. The shrine, still intact, now has a place of honor in my home.

Those, like myself, who follow her, believe that she is more approachable than Guadalupe. Santa Muerte is as basic as the earth around the graves she populates. She is organic and real. As one street merchant put it, "She gets us. She is a bitch like us." Another jokingly says that if you are in Mexico and you see a line of people outside a house, they are either selling tortillas or it is a Santa Muerte shrine.

Guadalupe is appropriately viewed as a miracle worker, while Santa Muerte is a problem-solver. Guadalupe is a distant holy mother and Santa Muerte is a saint of the people. She is the granter of favors and you can go to her crying the ugly cry and know that you will not be judged harshly (or at all), even if your own actions contributed to or were the sole cause of your downfall. She will systematically set about fixing what is broken, but once you put her in charge, it is best to get out of the way and not ask questions or second-guess the outcome.

Her magic is quick and very efficient, but does not always take the forms one expects. She brings endings to situations, and should only be petitioned when nothing less than the death of a debilitating circumstance required. Seek her out when you must definitively end something in your life. When you petition her, you must do so with the tremendous respect and reverence reserved for one who holds your death in her hands. You should also be ready, because she moves fast and there is no opportunity to take back what you set in motion with her. When you put a situation into her hands, she expects you to let go of it and trust her to handle it.

Bring her an offering. She revels in all forms of merriment and expressions of life, especially those that are sweet, salty, fun, or mind-altering. Because she is death, nothing can harm her, so she engages life to the fullest and encourages us, even in our fragile human state, to do the same, and to take not one moment for granted. This too is why the Church rejects and maligns her. She endorses the hedonistic, all-hands-on-deck life that Catholicism sought to squelch out.

Our Lady of Guadalupe, the Blessed Mother, is an intermediary between human beings and her son, Jesus Christ. Jesus Christ is the way to God, who the Bible represents as an overlord with human beings as servants to him. Jesus asks us to become "fishers of men" and to serve God. Santa Muerte, however, is the exact opposite. She works for people as a divine servant herself. She gets results very quickly and efficiently, but you must acquiesce to allow her to manage any situation you bring to her in her own way, on her terms.

To reiterate, be of complete and total conviction when you ask her for *anything;* however, you cannot stop her once she is in motion. If you promise her something, make certain you follow through. A strong aspect of Santa Muerte veneration is that of accountability, and she does not suffer fools lightly.

——— 18 ———
Brujería/Curanderismo Today

Unlike Granny Magic, which to all appearances is dying out, and Hoodoo, which achieved popularity for a niche audience of participants, Curanderismo and Brujería are flourishing, relatively unhindered by the cultural shifts and adjustments of the other two folk magic traditions we have discussed. Find any Mexican-American community in the United States and, with a bit of questioning, you will find a curandera and, if you are lucky, perhaps even a brujo.

Today, as in the past, the curandero is usually of the same socioeconomic standing as their clients, living in the same community and sharing the same lifestyle. Their clients are their neighbors, and as such, the curandera is highly accessible, with most practitioners working out of their home and requiring no appointments.

Always adaptable and eager to assimilate new healing modalities, both Curanderismo and Brujería now incorporate what many consider to be new age concepts such as crystal and gemstone healing, iridology, juicing, aura work, chakra alignment, Reiki, and color magic. Their tools of the trade remain easily attainable: herbs, stones, fruits, eggs, roots, and oils, most of which are local to the community. Their theology embraces the idea that indigenous, natural materials heal the ailments most likely to occur in that geographic area, hearkening back to the Mountain Magic idea that for every malady, God provides a cure.

So widespread is the awareness that Curanderismo is a valid and effective healing practice that many universities in Mexico and the southwestern United States offer classes in Mexican and Mexican-American healing practices.

Most brujas and curanderas make their own medicines and tools. They use Judeo-Christian symbolism as focus tools for themselves and their patients. The incantations are both scripture and ancient healing words. Their practice is an intricate dance of the old and the new, melded together in an ever-evolving, thriving practice. Just as their ancestors did, they heal using tinctures, salves, concoctions, poultices, and deep spiritual cleansings, both internal and external. Most work on the material level, but there are still practitioners who specialize in the mental and spiritual levels.

Unlike Hoodoo, very little written instruction is available about Curanderismo and Brujería, especially in English. Most books on the subject are sensationalized or written by outsiders with no understanding of the cultural context of the traditions. Many try to "Wiccanize" the practices, which does not work well. Brujería and Curanderismo are ceremonial and ritualized, but in a much different fashion than Wicca or other organized Pagan religions. The ceremony is personal and connects the practitioner and the client to God, or to a saint representing God, rather than calling in quarters, casting a circle, or invoking alternate deities. The brujo or curandero may invoke elemental energies, but this is usually done through physical representations of the element (stones, water, candles, incense) rather than an invocation of the unseen element.

In both practices, healers engage the supernatural. The consensus in the culture remains that brujos do so to harm, while curanderos do so to heal. And to some degree, that is accurate. A brujo has far less objection to harming another through supernatural means than do most who operate on that high of a spiritual level. That does not mean that they do so all the time, but merely that they can and will if the situation demands it, whereas a curandero engages supernatural energies with healing as the primary motivation. The exception is in a case of magical retribution, when a curandera will retaliate against a magical attack on behalf of a patient to facilitate a cure of presenting symptoms.

The overlapping of modalities is common in Brujería and Curanderismo. Either practitioner will without hesitation use a *sortilegio* (a conjure or spell) to contain harmful influences or an *amarre* (binding spell) to keep a spouse from wandering. They will stop an alcoholic husband from drink-ing the rent away on behalf of the desperate wife or force an employer to hire or promote one employee over another. They view this as healing the patient of their misfortune rather than any infraction of free will concepts.

When either a bruja or a curandera works with a patient or client, their focus and advocacy lie solely with the client and what best serves the client's ideal outcome. Sometimes this involves manipulating the behavior of people around the client. They consider all aspects of the client's well-being and environment, including their psychological and spiritual in-fluences, as well as their socio-cultural norms. All play a part in the composite self the healer evaluates to determine the form that treatment will take.

Limpias ... So Many Limpias

Within my own practice, the limpia is by far the most com-mon and interestingly, the most aggressive form of healing I use. A simple limpia uses only *salvia blanca* (white sage) or palo santo wood, and can relieve most issues. A sage stick is very reactive to the level of negativity in the environment, as well as its varying levels of concentration. Since I keep my home quite clean and "smudge" it out a minimum of once a day, when I light a sage stick, it usually burns low and emits a small amount of smoke. If an argument occurs or several people have been in and out of the house, the area might be mucky with negativity. This causes the sage to burn aggres-sively and the smoke rolls everywhere.

When I light a sage stick for a limpia, if the sage stick starts to billow smoke, I know the enthusiastic reaction from the sage is most likely related to the client standing in front of me. The behavior of the sage smoke helps me to determine right away the level of cleansing needed.

As I carry the smoldering sage stick over their body, front and back, I observe the areas of the body where the smoke dies down and where it increases. This marks places of imbalance and dis-ease on the physical or energetic level. As I do this, I speak to the client about what I see and sense during this preliminary process. "Are you having trouble with your periods?" "Do you have neck pain?" "Have you recently had symptoms of a bladder infection?" "Do you get migraines?"

Often, the limpia itself is sufficient to relieve the client's symptoms and heal the issue causing the problem. Cleansing the client with sage is curative and is also an effective and valuable diagnostic tool that may lead to other treatments. If the sage stick tells me the client has migraines, I know to treat with lots of lemon water and the application of lavender oil. Bladder issues mean plenty of cranberry juice or supplements, and again, gallons of lemon or lime water. If the sage stick reacts to one of the seven chakra points, I know we are working with a spiritual malady that is presenting as a physical malady. A reaction in the solar plexus means there are issues of unrequited love or a deep imbalance and unfairness in an interpersonal relationship. A reaction on the crown chakra means the person has insomnia or other sleep-related problems, stemming from their resistance to follow their own manifest destiny. They suffer because they are not living their own authentic life.

In many cases, especially for physical ailments without a strong spiritual or mental component, the initial saging is sufficient to start the healing process. I may also suggest other herbal remedies to speed up and continue the healing process we started in the shop.

When a spiritual component is in play or the client reports they are the victim of a curse or crossing, a deeper treatment is needed. When I worked solely in European-based Witch-craft, it was rare to come across a true cursing. People often *think* they are cursed, but it is unusual for their suspicions to be confirmed. More often, a series of unfortunate lapses in good judgment resulted in a string of misfortune that they presumed resulted from a supernatural attack.

In the Mexican-American community, however, if some-one tells you they have been cursed, believe them. They likely were. In all cases in which a client in the Mexican-American community tells me directly that someone worked against them, I immediately begin treatment under the presumption that this is true.

I start with the basic sage limpia, but then move on to more aggressive work. The next step is the use of a ritual blade to cut away any attachments from the curse sent to the client. I trace around the body with the blade, cutting through areas of denseness where the curse took hold. Often, it takes two or more passes with the blade to disconnect all the tentacles and hooks of the spell. I do candle-work with crucitas (little crosses) to further heal areas of attachment, almost like a spiritual cauterization of the "wound" where the spell attached to the client, while reciting an incantation to ward off evil and force the spell entity to leave the immediate environment and return to its sender, whoever that may be. Asperging with holy water furthers the cleansing and healing processes and connects the client's spirit back into their body, the belief being that when the client experiences trauma, the spirit temporarily leaves the physical form that is undergoing the trauma. This is also part of the treatment process for a *susto,* and many healers believe the partial or complete vacancy of spirit is the cause of many forms of mental illness.

I massage the client with an egg or a lime to extract any remaining effects of the curse left within the body or spirit, again while speaking a healing and extracting incantation. I then sweep the body with an herb bundle (*barrida*) that further heals, and I follow up with a magical spray that works like a "setting spray" to finalize the cleansing and bless the client. My favorite is "*Las Siete Potencias*" (The Seven African Powers). The final step is to light the sage stick again and conduct a complete recheck to locate areas that still register with the sage stick as troublesome. If necessary, we start all over again and repeat the process until the client reads as clean and clear.

I advise the client to treat the next week as though they are recovering from the flu: lots of rest, lots of liquids, and no heavy lifting or exertion. Self-care is important after a complete spiritual cleansing. Sometimes, if the negative energy has affected them for a long time, they will either sleep an unusual amount while their body continues to heal, or they will feel so good with their energy field cleaned that they overdo things and take on too much at once.

Although limpias are by far my most used healing practice, candle work is the second. This is done using a glass-encased novena candle and a prescribed prayer the client recites for nine days while burning the candle. The work follows the moon phases, banishing during the waning moon and manifesting or drawing in during the waxing moon. I treat the candle with an infusion of sympathetic oils, followed by an herbal mix supportive of the goal. The client recites a traditional novena prayer, or I write a customized one tailored to their specific need. If a client's need is strong, I may have them burn the candle all at once in a five-day run rather than a little at a time over nine days.

Because I am the last recourse for many people in desperate situations, I quickly learned to keep a large supply of tissues on hand. Men and women alike shed tears, and I often do as well.

In today's practice, the primary difference between the curandera and the bruja, aside from the associated social stigma, is that the curandera is exclusively a healer who uses herbs and incantations to heal a client on all levels. The curandera treats everything, ranging from bedwetting to spiritual possession. The bruja works with all types of spiritual healing as well as some physical healing, but their primary focus is on the supernatural processes, whether there is physical manifestation or not.

—— 19 ——
Brujería/Curanderismo Charms and Spells

Of all the folk magic systems within the scope of this book, Brujería and Curanderismo are by far the most elusive. The scarcity of printed work, and even less written in English, regarding the two healing systems belies a wide expanse of techniques and magical processes spanning more than two thousand years of developmental history. Because a Bruja or Curandera learns through an intensive apprenticeship process, most lessons take place in the moment and are not a matter of book study. Instead, the learning and training happens experientially. As such, there are not as many direct spells to share as there are in Granny Magic, whose practices we might now refer to as "old wives tales" and "superstitions," or as in Hoodoo with its many recipes for washes, oils, and powders. If the reader feels drawn to Brujería and Curanderismo, I recommend they find a qualified teacher to act as their mentor. Here, however, are a few techniques and incantations that Mexican folk magic practitioners commonly use.

Aceite de Serpiente de Cascabel (Rattlesnake Oil)

Unlike the snake oil salesman who peddled bogus Hoodoo products to unsuspecting villagers, in Curanderismo, actual snake oil, rendered from rattlesnake fat, is used in salves and soaps. Rarely is this product available commercially, but if you are fortunate enough to find an authentic healer who makes their own version, be sure to stock up. It is a very effective remedy for very nearly any inflammatory condition, including arthritis, gout, muscle pain, and even acne.

La Piedra de Iman (Lodestone)

Lodestones are natural magnets fed by iron filings, and, used correctly, they bring good luck, harmony, balance, and draw in what the client needs. They are carried in a small bag and treated as living entities. Red lodestones draw in love, and green stones draw in money and financial stability. Lodestones are social creatures and prefer to work in pairs. They love gifts and welcome them to their bag home. To increase the draw for money, offer a gold bead as a gift to the lodestone and keep it in the bag alongside it. Offer a silver bead to bring harmony to the home, a copper penny to bring wealth to the poor, a red bead to purge envy, and a wire bent in the shape of a horseshoe to bring good fortune.

Los Siete Nudos (The Seven Knots)

Think of seven problems you need to solve and sit with two feet of red ribbon in front of you. Focus on each problem individually and tie a knot in the ribbon for each problem. Start with a knot in the exact middle of the ribbon for problem number one. Next, tie a knot approximately four inches to the left of the first, then a third knot approximately four inches to the right of the first. Your fourth and fifth knots are tied approximately four inches out from the second and third, and the sixth may go on either side that you choose. The seventh knot ties one end of the ribbon to the other end, binding the problems into the ribbon so that they may no longer harm you. Place the ribbon circle into a jar and bury it far from you where it will not be broken or disturbed. Tradition states that you must do so alone and that no one may see you bury the jar or the spell will be broken.

Encourage Good Sleep

Make a cross of large sage springs. The leaves may be attached or not. Place the cross under your pillow to ward off evil spirits and encourage restful, restorative sleep. Use for only three nights, then bury the cross at a crossroads and replace it with a new one.

Childbirth Magic

Place a gold coin over a newborn's umbilicus and bind it with a clean, white cotton cloth to protect the child against evil influences.

A baby born or conceived during a lunar eclipse is thought likely to have a cleft palate. A pregnant woman must not allow any metal objects, such as a necklace, coins, etc., touch her belly during a lunar eclipse because this combination of factors is suspected to cause cleft palate.

Throughout history, *parteras* knew that health of both mother and baby depended on the mother's diet and insisted on the elimination of all impurities in what the pregnant woman ate or drank. For forty days following childbirth, the postnatal mother must lift nothing heavier than her baby, must not bend or exert herself, and may not have sexual intercourse. Fifteen days after birth, she experiences a *temezcalli,* which is a sweat lodge purification ceremony using purified water treated with rue, basil, and rosemary that is then poured onto hot stones. This heals strained muscles and restores health and life to her body tissues.

Agua Bendita (Holy Water)

Holy water is an all-purpose, spiritual cleansing product and is a direct connector between the spirit and the Divine, as well as a means to rejoin a wandering spirit back to the body where it belongs. In our area, agua bendita is seasonal, and if we run out, we run out. We consider it an essential product in our shop and our practice, but we care enough about the quality of the product that we feel it must be made correctly or not at all.

Agua bendita is made solely from rainwater caught and cured in a copper vessel. A silver bullion is placed in the bowl of water, along with a stick of *palo santo* (holy wood) to allow the silver and palo to permeate the water. After the water is well infused, it is then exposed to sunlight to gather the energies of light into it.

Holy water is used to asperge the patient during healing or as an anointing product.

El Credo de los Apóstoles (The Apostles' Creed)

The Apostles' Creed is the oldest creed of the Christian Church and dates back to at least 140 CE. It is one of the most commonly used recitations for healings. Both brujas and curanderas engage it to heal on either the material, mental, or spiritual level. It is generally recited three times and should be memorized and spoken by rote rather than read. When reciting it, the healer infuses the words with absolute faith in and veneration of God, Jesus, the Holy Spirit, and the Virgin Mary. When in doubt about what incantation to use for healing, use the Apostles' Creed:

I believe in God, the Father almighty, creator of Heaven and earth. I believe in Jesus Christ, God's only Son, our Lord, who was conceived by the Holy Spirit, born of the Virgin Mary, suffered under Pontius Pilate, was crucified, died, and was buried; he descended to the dead.

On the third day he rose again; he ascended into Heaven, he is seated at the right hand of the Father, and he will come to judge the living and the dead. I believe in the Holy Spirit, the holy Catholic Church,

the communion of saints, the forgiveness of sins,
the resurrection of the body, and the life everlasting.
Amen.

Las Doce Verdades de Mundo
(The Twelve Truths of the World)

This prayer is most often used by brujas and brujos, giving
it the shadow name of the "Witches' Prayer," even though it
is clearly quite religious in nature. Some healers recite the
twelve truths of the world in ascending order and others in
descending order. When the prayer starts with one truth
rather than twelve, the process is called "building the Temple
of Jerusalem." We use the twelve truths of the world almost
exclusively for exorcisms.

A lead healer and their assistant use a specialized technique while reciting the twelve truths. It is essential that the
two people working this process have experience working together and an existing and strong spiritual bond or else the
incantation can take a dangerous turn. When done correctly,
this incantation challenges a demon or devil that has possessed the victim and forces it out of the body.

The lead healer stands in front of the client and the assistant stands behind. Both hold cleansing agents such as palo
santo or sage and work in tandem cleansing the body. The
words of the incantation act as a challenge for the resident
demon/devil and are delivered in a call and response fashion
with the lead healer saying the first part of each line and the
assistant answering for the demon, as shown below:

Lead healer: "Of the twelve truths of the world, give me one."

Assistant healer: "God, Christ, who came down to bless the Holy House of Jerusalem."

Lead healer: "Of the twelve truths of the world, give me two."

Assistant healer: "The two tablets of Moses."

The full twelve truths are worked in this fashion.

Often, partway through the process—which can take several repetitions and many cleanses, sometimes ongoing for hours—the client will collapse backward. The assistant must remain alert and remain prepared to catch the client if they fall.

The client may thrash about, make odd noises, rage, curse, foam at the mouth, cry out, speak in odd cadence or dialects, weep, shake, have intense chills, or sweat profusely. Once the process begins, it is essential that the two healers continue through to full completion. Failure to finish the healing once it begins can endanger both the client and the healers. Clearly, this intervention is ill-advised for healers without the appropriate experience and expertise to manage it correctly.

There are many versions of the twelve truths of the world, sometimes using different "truths" for the response section. In its written form below, I include commentary on each line. Unbolded words are not part of the prayer but are explanations for any who may not be Christian-literate. Both the call and the appropriate response are listed below.

Of the twelve truths of the world, tell me one.
God, Christ, who came down to bless the Holy House of Jerusalem. (The one God. Alternately, the one truth is sometimes "The Holy House of Jerusalem.")

Of the twelve truths of the world, tell me two.
The two tablets of Moses. (The two tablets on which Moses received the Ten Commandments.)

Of the twelve truths of the world, tell me three.
The Holy Trinity. (God the Father, Jesus the Son, and the Holy Spirit. This truth is sometimes represented as "The Three Marys" meaning Mary the mother, Mary Magdalene, and Mary, the sister of Martha and Lazarus.)

Of the twelve truths of the world, tell me four.
The four evangelists. (Matthew, Mark, Luke, and John.)

Of the twelve truths of the world, tell me five.
The five wounds. (Wounds of the crucifixion of Christ: one in each foot, one in each hand, and the wound where the Roman soldier's spear pierced His side to make certain he was dead.)

Of the twelve truths of the world, tell me six.
The six candelabras. (This refers to the six candles that burned in Galilee or the six candles lit for a High Mass in Catholicism.)

Of the twelve truths of the world, tell me seven.
The seven words. (References seven statements of Christ on the cross rather than seven individual words.)

Of the twelve truths of the world, tell me eight.
The eight anguishes. (The eight anguishes of Mary, the Blessed Mother. In some versions, the response is "the eight joys.")

Of the twelve truths of the world, tell me nine.
The nine months of Mary. (The months of her pregnancy.)

Of the twelve truths of the world, tell me ten.
The Ten Commandments. (The words written on the two tablets of Moses.)

Of the twelve truths of the world, tell me eleven.
The eleven thousand virgins. (References the "Golden Legend" of Saint Ursula and the 11,000 Virgins.)

Of the twelve truths of the world, tell me twelve.
The twelve apostles who accompanied our Lord on the cross.

Amen

Sometimes, a thirteenth truth is added:

Of the twelve truths of the world, tell me thirteen.
The Thirteen Rays of the Sun that send witches and wizards to hell, so it shall be God the Father, God the Son, and God the Holy Spirit, forever and ever.

When the entire process is over and the lead healer is satisfied that the demon or devil is removed or contained, they will usually perform a soul-retrieval ceremony to make certain the soul is well within the body and prepared to heal from the experience of possession. The healer then prepares any written instructions for them to take as they leave. The experience is exhausting and sometimes nerve-wracking for all concerned.

Once the client leaves, the lead healer usually prays a rosary or uses some other form of spiritual bonding to cleanse away any impurities transferred into them by the process. Some healers expectorate black or bloodied mucus for an hour or so after completion of the ritual. Since the lead healer is pulling the entity from the client and the assistant is speaking on behalf of the entity, the lead healer often endures the worst of the experience. The assistant, however, should also go through extensive cleansing and spiritual rehabilitating themselves afterward. The assistant is also frequently sore throughout their body from the physical effort of supporting the client.

The entity is usually contained in a sealed jar, an amulet, or an egg, then buried or otherwise contained in a location where it cannot be disturbed.

Crossroads of Conjure

The world of Conjure practice escapes the attention of many souls and calls like a siren to others. I am blessed to have experienced not just one of the vibrant Conjure practices covered in this book, but all three of them. I did not merely study them from a removed, academic perspective, but lived in each of them.

Conjure came to me when I was an older Witch who thought there was nothing new under the sun … not for me, anyway. I worked as a Wiccan high priestess for over a decade. My husband and I created our own rewarding spiritual path, CUSP, and its generous nature allows it to function independently or to blend seamlessly with any other spiritual tradition. It became a comfortable home for me and I thought it was where I would stay.

Over time, I noticed that the magical practices that came very naturally to me were nothing like those of the other

Wiccans I knew. I am comfortable with being the oddball in any group, so I thought nothing of it until a friend of mine, Wulf, who seems to be instrumental in many of my most significant life changes, pulled me aside and said, "You need to study Conjure. It is important."

I asked him why. I was perfectly content with my existing path and my arrogance that I had learned all I needed to know clouded the enthusiasm I might otherwise have shown at learning something new.

"Because it is *who you are* and it is *what you are already doing*," he replied.

Things happened quickly after that. They say that when the student is ready, the teacher will come, and right away, mentors appeared as if by magic. After decades of magical practice, I was busted down to a novice again, but the information and techniques I learned felt organic and familiar. I learned quickly...or I guess I should say that I remembered quickly.

Since I left Kentucky in 1978, I thought little about the magical practices I knew growing up. I was eager to leave my country home behind and see the world, and those memories were part of what I left behind. As my study of Conjure continued, that incredible cache of cultural and ancestral lore came back to me in a flood.

In the case of Granny Magic, it was like doors blew open in my mind. "Yes, I've done this." "I have done this as well." "Yes, we did this."

Hoodoo came easy to me. The British Witches with whom I trained in the early 1980s became frustrated with me over time because of my complete inability to keep herb names straight. They all looked like weeds to me, and my teachers would throw up their hands in dismay because I could not learn or retain their herbal language.

The roots, flowers, and barks of Hoodoo practice, however, were so familiar to me that I could correctly name them just by touching them. For twenty years, I thought I had no proclivity for herbs because of my early experiences, when it was simply a matter of getting me into the environment that grew the herbs I instinctively knew. The words, the scriptures, the incantations were all locked away in my mind and the keys of Conjure unlocked them and reminded me not only of what I did not know, but of what I *did* know.

That is not to say I did not have a great deal to learn. Patient teachers and mentors worked with me, answering my many questions with grace and correcting my many errors. Some of my mentors I named in this text, and some prefer to remain closeted.

After Hoodoo came Curanderismo, and in my experience, the study became a long drop down a rabbit hole that I have no interest in escaping. Along with Curanderismo came total immersion in the magical life.

Every spiritual path I have followed in my life remains with me today and informs not only how I practice, but who I am in the world.

I was raised as a devout Christian surrounded by folk magic and superstition. I found Paganism and it addressed needs inside me that found no solace anywhere else.

Rootworking/Hoodoo got my hands dirty. As Maya Grey puts it, "where your hands and feet are in mud, bone, smoke, and whiskey." Hoodoo taught me about service to others in a way that no spiritual path had done before. It also taught me about the false prisons we assign to ourselves when we accept the theologies and dogmas created to control us through fear. Hoodoo taught me something that spoke to my spirit in a way Christianity and Wicca did not. It said that there comes a time when we no longer must passively turn the other cheek and wait for karma to kick in, and that sometimes, we ourselves must be the instrument of our own deliverance out of oppression.

Brujería and Curanderismo took me to the next level and showed me not only how to live in service to others, but how to go to the mat for them, how to throw down in the magical arena and give beyond what you believe your magical limits to be.

This was my progression, and each person will have their own experience under that broad and beautiful umbrella of Conjure, if they are called into its practice. I feel blessed to stand at the crossroads of Conjure, influenced strongly by each of these three folk magic systems. Each one defines me in some way.

As some of these paths fade away more with each passing day, threatening to wink out of existence, I remind myself that, above all, in nature there are cycles. What was once old is now new and what was gone returns in an ever-shifting dance of progress forward. Now we enjoy a return to the Conjure practices that address basic needs and, above all, personal accountability. I am honored to be a part of this time and the practice of Conjure.

If you are called to do so, I hope that you will join me at the crossroads of Conjure and find the practice that resonates in your spirit.

GLOSSARY

African Diaspora: Communities throughout the world created initially by the historical movement of the indigenous peoples of Africa to America and other places around the world, primarily through slave trade activities. (Hoodoo)

African Traditional Religions (ATR): The indigenous religions of the African people, including their cosmology, ritual practices, symbols, arts, and society, as well as their culture and worldview, since no delineation between these concepts existed. (Hoodoo)

Amarre: A binding spell. (Curanderismo & Brujería)

Animism: The belief that every physical item, living and non-living, possesses a soul and its own distinct spiritual essence.

Asperge: To sprinkle holy water or a sacred wash onto a client or ritual tool for purposes of ritual purification.

Barrida: A ritual cleansing that involves sweeping the body with an herb bundle or actual broom. (Curanderismo & Brujería)

Bibliomancy: The use of books for divinatory purposes.

Bilis: A condition caused by unresolved and suppressed anger. (Curanderismo & Brujería)

Black Belt Hoodoo: The first phase of Hoodoo, originating in the earliest African American plantation slave communities.

Black Codes: Oppressive laws passed in the post-Emancipation Southern United States discriminating against freed people of color and keeping them from any reasonable quality of life.

Botánica: A shop selling spiritual supplies, often run by a brujo or curandera.

Bottle Trees: Multi-colored glass bottles hung onto a tree or slid onto the branches through the bottle neck, believed to repel evil spirits from the home (Granny Magic & Hoodoo)

Bruja: A female witch. (Brujería)

Brujería: Witchcraft.

Brujo: A male witch. (Brujería)

Cajun: Descendants of the French-Canadians living in the bayou areas of Southern Louisiana. (Hoodoo)

Cascarilla: Powdered eggshell used to create protective boundaries. (Hoodoo & Brujería)

Caul: The amniotic membrane that covers a baby's face at birth if the membranes do not rupture spontaneously before or as the baby is expelled from the mother's body.

Chakra Points: Seven energy point, in a line from the tailbone to the top of the head, each with charge over a specific life force.

Charivari: A ribald celebration involving putting a new bride and groom to bed and then making a great deal of noise to cover the sounds of their lovemaking as the marriage is consummated. (Granny Magic)

Chewing the Root: A spell performed by qualified conjure doctors, primarily to resolve legal matters in the client's favor. The conjure doctor sits in the courtroom and chews on galangal root while focusing energy toward the positive outcome of the legal matter. (Hoodoo)

Concoction: A mixture of various ingredients or elements.

Conjure: A broad term applying to various magical practices that use herbal and root products combined with spiritual incantations and energy work. It is most commonly associated with Hoodoo or Rootworking, but also includes Brujería and Granny Magic.

Conjure Doctor: A Hoodoo practitioner specializing in spiritual and magical work rather than pharmacopeia-based healing.

Creole: A person of mixed European and African descent. (Hoodoo)

Crossing Powder: A compound intended to levy a curse or hex against a person. (Hoodoo)

Crossroads: A sacred place where two roads join. If the two roads cross over one another, it is a female crossroads, and if they fork away from one another, it is a male crossroads. The crossroads is a strongly magical location in nearly all folk magic paths.

Crucitas: Meaning "small crosses," this term refers to using a candle to trace tiny cross shapes onto the body of a client to encourage healing. (Curanderismo & Brujería)

Cunning-Folk: The European folk healers, particularly of Ireland and Scotland. (Granny Magic)

Curandera: A female healer and practitioner of Curanderismo.

Curanderismo: The Mexican tradition of healing, based on Mayan, Aztec, and Spanish modalities.

Curandero: A male healer and practitioner of Curanderismo.

Decoction: The substance containing the concentrated essence of plant matter that remains after it is heated or boiled, usually for medicinal purposes.

Doll Babies: Roughly fashioned human figures used in Hoodoo as a proxy for the individual for or on whom the spell is worked.

Dowsing Rod: A tool used to detect water, minerals, or lost items beneath the earth's surface. (Granny Magic)

Dung: Animal manure.

Empacho: A condition caused by a blockage somewhere in the digestive tract. (Curanderismo)

Fictive Kin: A technique used to engender an undeserved familiarity with the target of an advertising campaign through words such as "brother" and "sister." (Marketeered Hoodoo)

Fidencistas: Followers of El Niño Fidencio, a famous Mexican healer later canonized by the Catholic Church. (Curanderismo)

Folk Magic: A set of magical practices generally used by the common people of an area.

Goofer Dust: A substance used to remove problem people from a specific area. (Hoodoo)

Goomer Doctor: A practitioner of Mountain Magic who specializes in the use of charms, incantations, and energy movement. (Granny Magic)

Granny Doctor: A practitioner of Mountain Magic who specializes in the treatment of physical disease, midwifery, and injury. (Granny Magic)

Granny Magic: The umbrella term used to encompass Mountain Magic, particularly of healing and charms.

Granny Woman: A woman who practices Mountain Magic. (Granny Magic)

Graveyard Dirt: Dirt collected from the grave areas of a cemetery for magical use. (Used in all three forms of Conjure covered in this book.)

Great Awakenings (or Great Revival): A series of evangelical Christian meetings which began in Logan County, Kentucky and spread throughout the American South from 1800–1801. Credited as the beginning of the Bible Belt, the Great Revival was a surge of Protestant religious fervor. (Granny Magic)

Great Migration: The movement of six million African Americans, between 1916 and 1970, out of the rural Southern United States to the urban Northeast, Midwest, and West. (Hoodoo)

Gris Gris: A small cloth bag containing magical items intended to bring good fortune or specialized fortune (love, health, money) to the carrier. (New Orleans Hoodoo/Voodoo)

Haint Blue: A light blue periwinkle color used to paint the inside roof of an enclosed porch or entryway. The color is believed to repel evil spirits and ghosts. (Hoodoo/Granny Magic)

Holy Trinity: The combined spiritual essences of the Father, Son, and Holy Spirit/Holy Ghost. (Christianity)

Holy Water (Agua Bendita): Water made using rainwater infused with silver and palo santo, applied through asperging or anointing. (Brujería)

Honeypot: A spell in which personal items are placed in a jar of honey, syrup, or sugar water to "sweeten" a relationship. (Hoodoo)

Hoodoo: A magical practice developed out of the spiritual and healing techniques of African slaves in the American South. Hoodoo has components of French, Cajun, Haitian, Native American, and Mountain Magic practices in its modern presentation.

Hot Foot Powder: A compound used to "light a fire under" the target and motivate them into the desired action. (Hoodoo)

Hueseros: A curandero who treats bone fractures. (Curanderismo)

Iridology: A medical practice in which the iris of the eye is studied for certain color and pattern presentations.

Jack: Short for "Jack Ball," this is a magical charm that is fixed into a small ball that is carried on your person for luck. (Hoodoo)

Jaculatoria: A short, intense prayer. (Curanderismo & Brujería)

Laying Tricks: Casting spells. (Hoodoo)

Limpia: A ritual cleansing using the smoke of burning herbs, as well as eggs, lemons, limes, herb bundles, candles, and sprays. (Curanderismo & Brujería)

Lodestone (La Piedra de Iman): Natural magnets used to draw an item or person to the target (Brujería, Curanderismo & Hoodoo)

Lwa/Loa: The sacred spirits and pantheon of Haitian Vodou and Louisiana Voodoo.

Lych: *Pronounced "litch."* A corpse. (Granny Magic)

Lying In: A time after death when a lych stays in the family home so mourners may view the body. (Granny Magic)

Mal Aire: Literally interprets as "bad air," mal aire is a condition caused by taking in chilled or night air. (Curanderismo & Brujería)

Marketeered Hoodoo: A term coined by Katrina Hazzard-Donald referring to the commercialization of Hoodoo products targeted at the African Americans who relocated to the American North following the Emancipation. (Hoodoo)

Material Level (Nivel Material): Working with Curanderismo using physical tools such as herbs, candles, stones, and focus tools. (Curanderismo & Brujería)

Matrilineal: Tracing lineage through the mother's family line rather than the father's.

Mental Level (Nivel Mental): Working with Curanderismo through mental focus (Curanderismo & Brujería)

Mercury Dime: A ten-cent coin struck by the United States Mint from 1916 to 1945. (Hoodoo)

Mojo Bag: A cloth bag containing magical items directed toward a specific desired outcome. Similar to a Gris Gris. (Hoodoo)

Muina: A condition resulting from explosive rages and outwardly directed anger. (Curanderismo & Brujería)

Nature Sack: A magical sack a woman secretly ties during coitus, designed to control a specific man's virility. (Hoodoo)

New Orleans Voodoo: A branch of Hoodoo that combined African spiritual and healing techniques with French, Creole, Cajun, and Haitian magical practices. (Hoodoo)

Novena: A concerted prayer repeated over nine days, usually in conjunction with candle work. (Hoodoo, Curanderismo, Brujería)

Omen: A natural and observed occurrence that is unusual, such as unusual behavior in plants or animals. (Granny Magic)

Oracionistas: Curanderos who work primarily through the power of focused prayer. (Curanderismo & Brujería)

Pagan: One who does not follow the Christian religions. A Pagan is usually polytheistic and venerates natural expressions of the Divine.

Palo Santo: The wood from a tree in Central America that emanates strong cleansing and protective properties when burned or infused. (Curanderismo & Brujería)

Pantheism: A religious practice involving the worship of plural, interconnected gods.

Partera: A curandera who specializes in midwifery. (Curanderismo & Brujería)

Penal Laws: Oppressive laws passed in Ireland in the 1700s attempting to force Irish Roman Catholics and Protestant dissenters to accept the English-state established Anglican Church. (Granny Magic)

Pilgrimage: A religious journey.

Plática: A detailed therapeutic consultation conducted with a client by a brujo or curandero. (Brujería & Curanderismo)

Poppets: Similar to Hoodoo doll babies, poppets are fabric, human-shaped figures used in spellwork. The user fills the poppet with sympathetic herbs and identifying items and uses the poppet as a proxy for the target of their magic. (Hoodoo)

Poultice: A soft, moist mass of medicinal herbs or other plant or organic matter, applied to an afflicted area of the body, and held in place with bandaging.

Power Doctor: A Mountain Magic healer specializing in the use of charms, incantations, and spiritual energy movement for healing and manifesting desired outcomes. Similar to the conjure doctor in Hoodoo. (Granny Magic)

Pow-wow: A system of folk magic based on the spiritual practices of the Pennsylvania Dutch.

Rattlesnake Oil (Aceite de Serpiente de Cascabel): A salve or treatment made from the rendered fat of a rattlesnake, used to treat inflammatory diseases, arthritis, gout, depression, and acne, among other things. (Curanderismo & Brujería)

Reconstruction Era: The time following the United States Civil War from 1865–1877.

Red Brick Dust: Finely processed dust created by the intentional break down of red clay bricks. Used to create protective boundaries. (Hoodoo)

Reflexology: An alternative medicine practice involving the use of pressure on specific points of the hands and feet.

Root Doctor: A Hoodoo rootworker specializing in herbal healing practices. (Hoodoo)

Rootworker: A universal name for someone who practices Hoodoo. (Hoodoo)

Salve: An ointment, usually handmade, used to promote the healing of skin and/or to convey the healing properties of oil or herbs to an area.

Scotch-Irish: Immigrants of Scottish and Irish descent who came to the Appalachian and Ozark Mountain areas from Ulster in Ireland. (Granny Magic)

Seer: A person who is psychic or has other gifts of prophecy or foresight. (Granny Magic)

Sign: A naturally occurring and observable change that instructs a behavior, such as planting a certain crop when specific trees bloom. (Granny Magic)

Sin Eater: A figure in Mountain Magic and European history who comes to a home upon the death of a person and takes on their unconfessed and unforgiven sins by eating food that rested on or passed over their body immediately before or after death. (Granny Magic)

Skyclad: Performing magical work in the nude. (Wicca)

Sobadores: A curandera who works on the material level and specializes in sprained muscles, ligaments, and tissue damage, sometimes through massage. (Curanderismo & Brujería)

Sortilegio: A magical spell or enchantment, most commonly for love. (Curanderismo & Brujería)

Spanish Conquistadors: The Spanish invaders who conquered the Aztec Nation, in this case led by Hernán Cortés (Curanderismo & Brujería)

Spiritual Level (Nivel Espiritual): Curanderas who work solely with spiritual energy to heal. (Curanderismo & Brujería)

Susto: A magical fright, similar to post-traumatic stress syndrome. (Curanderismo & Brujería)

Syncretization: The assimilation of one spiritual practice onto another dominant one, usually to allow continuation of the first practice under the guise of the second.

Temezcalli: A therapeutic sweat lodge practice (Curanderismo & Brujería)

The Evil Eye (Mal de Ojo): A condition caused by one person looking upon another with great admiration or envy without physically touching them to discharge that emotion. (Curanderismo & Brujería)

Tilma: A cloak made of cactus fibers. (Curanderismo & Brujería)

Tincture: A liquid extract for healing, made from herbs soaked in alcohol or vinegar and taken orally.

Traiteur: A Creole faith healer. (Hoodoo)

Transatlantic Slave Trade: The segment of the slave trade operating between the sixteenth and nineteenth centuries, responsible for transporting between ten and twelve million enslaved Africans across the Atlantic Ocean to the Americas.

Two-Headed Doctor: A Hoodoo doctor who healed using both herbal treatments and charms. (Hoodoo & Granny Magic)

Ulster-Irish: The Scotch-Irish immigrants who came to the Appalachian and Ozark Mountain areas from Ulster in Ireland. (Granny Magic)

Urban Hoodoo: An informal name for Hoodoo as it presents in a modern context, post-Marketeering era. (Hoodoo)

Vinegar Pot: Similar to a honeypot, a vinegar pot involves placing identifying items into a jar filled with vinegar and/or human urine to sour a relationship. (Hoodoo)

Voodoo/Vodou/VooDou/Voudoo: A set of spiritual practices based on the African Traditional Religions developed throughout Haiti and Louisiana, incorporating Creole traditions.

Water Witcher: A dowser who uses a pendulum or dowsing rod to locate water below the earth's surface. (Granny Magic)

Wiccan: A follower of the Pagan path of Wicca, created by Gerald Gardner.

Witch Ball: A ball of wax, human or animal hair, fingernails, teeth, and other personal items flung at a victim to curse them. (Granny Magic)

Witch Master: A power doctor who specializes in counter-acting the effects of witchcraft and the punishment of witches. (Granny Magic)

Witch Wiggler: A dowser who uses a pendulum or dows-ing rod to locate water below the earth's surface. A water witcher. (Granny Magic)

Yarb Doctor: From the term "herb doctor," a yarb doctor heals using herbs and is the male counterpart to a granny doctor. (Granny Magic)

Yerberos: A curandero who heals on the material level using herbal medicines. (Curanderismo & Brujería)

Bibliography

Accilien, Cécile, Jessica Adams, and Elmide Méléance (editors). 2006. *Revolutionary Freedoms: A History of Survival, Strength and Imagination in Haiti.* Coconut Creek, FL: Caribbean Studies Press.

Aptheker, Herbert. 1978. *American Negro Slave Revolts.* New York: International Publishers Co.

Asante, Molefi Kete. 2009. *Encyclopedia of African Religion.* Thousand Oaks, CA: SAGE Publications.

Avila, Elena and Joy Parker. 2000. *Woman Who Glows in the Dark: A Curandera Reveals Traditional Aztec Secrets of Physical and Spiritual Health.* New York: Jeremy P. Tarcher/Putnam.

Ballard, H. Byron. 2012. *Staubs and Ditchwater: A Friendly and Useful Introduction to Hillfolks' Hoodoo.* Asheville, NC: Silver Rings Press.

Barnett, Ronald A. 2009. "Our Lady of Guadalupe: Tonantzin or the Virgin Mary?" Mexconnect. http://www

.mexconnect.com/articles/2614-our-lady-of-guadalupe-tonantzin-or-the-virgin-mary.

Battad, Do. 2012. " Miraculous Image of Our Lady of Guadalupe." *Infallible Catholic* (blog). http://infallible-catholic.blogspot.com/2012/04/miraculous-image-of-our-lady-of.html.

Bird, Stephanie Rose. 2004. *Sticks, Stones, Roots & Bones: Hoodoo, Mojo & Conjuring with Herbs*. St. Paul, MN: Llewellyn Publications.

Bonewits, Isaac. 1989. *Real Magic: An Introductory Treatise on the Basic Principles of Yellow Magic*. York Beach, ME: Samuel Weiser.

Brown, Stacy. "Considering Curanderismo: The Place of Traditional Hispanic Folk Healing in Modern Medicine." ETHOS. Accessed October 5, 2017. (no longer available)

Chesnut, R. Andrew. 2012. *Devoted to Death: Santa Muerte, the Skeleton Saint*. New York, NY: Oxford University Press.

Chireau, Yvonne P. 1997. "Conjure and Christianity in the Nineteenth Century: Religious Elements in African American Magic." *Religion and American Culture 7*, no. 2: 225-246. https://www.jstor.org/stable/1123979?seq=1#page_scan_tab_contents.

———. 2003. *Black Magic: Religion and the African American Conjuring Tradition*. Berkeley, CA: University of California Press.

De La Torre, Miguel A. (editor). 2009. *Hispanic American Religious Cultures*. Santa Barbara, CA: ABC-CLIO.

Doyle Burns, Phyllis. 2018. "Granny Women: Healing and Magic in Appalachia." Remedy Grove. https://remedy-grove.com/traditional/grannywomenhealingandmagic.

Dunaway, Wilma A. 2008. *Women, Work and Family in the Antebellum Mountain South*. New York: Cambridge University Press.

Fett, Sharla M. 2002. *Working Cures: Healing, Health, and Power on Southern Slave Plantations*. Chapel Hill, NC: The University of North Carolina Press.

Foster, Susan. 2014. "Byron Ballard keeps Appalachian folk magic practices alive." *Mountain Xpress,* December 17, 2014. https://mountainx.com/living/wellness/byron-ballard-keeps-appalachian-folk-magic-practices-alive/.

Foxwood, Orion. 2012. *The Candle and the Crossroads: A Book of Appalachian Conjure and Southern Root Work*. San Francisco: Weiser Books.

———. 2015. *The Flame in the Cauldron: A Book of Old-Style Witchery*. San Francisco: Weiser Books.

Gardner, Gerald B. 2004. *The Meaning of Witchcraft*. York Beach, ME: Weiser Books.

González-Wippler, Migene. 2010. *Santeria: the Religion: Faith, Rites, Magic*. Woodbury, MN: Llewellyn Publications.

Guild, June Purcell. 2011. *Black Laws of Virginia: A Summary of the Legislative Acts of Virginia Concerning Negroes from*

Earliest Times to the Present. Westminster, MD: Heritage Books.

Hazzard-Donald, Katrina. 2013. *Mojo Workin': The Old African American Hoodoo System.* Chicago: University of Illinois Press.

Hohman, Johann Georg. 2008. *The Long-Lost Friend.* University Park, PA: Pennsylvania State University Press.

Hurston, Zora Neale. 1931. "Hoodoo in America," Journal of American Folklore 44, no.174: 317–417. https://www.jstor.org/stable/535394.

———. 2009. *Moses, Man of the Mountain.* New York: Harper Perennial.

———. 2008. *Mules and Men.* New York: Harper Perennial.

———. 1990. *Tell My Horse: Voodoo and Life in Haiti and Jamaica.* New York: Harper & Row.

Hyatt, Harry M. 1978. *Hoodoo – Conjuration – Witchcraft - Rootwork.* Cambridge, MD: Western Publishing Co..

Kuna, Ralph R. 1977. "Hoodoo: The Indigenous Medicine and Psychiatry of the Black American." *Mankind Quarterly* 18: 137-151.

Long, Carolyn Morrow. 2016. "Voudou." *Encyclopedia of Louisiana*, edited by David Johnson. http://www.knowlouisiana.org/entry/voudou.

Mar, Alex. 2015. *Witches of America.* New York: Sarah Crichton Books, Farrar, Straus and Giroux.

Matthews, Holly F. 1987. "Rootwork: Description of an Ethnomedical System in the American South," *Southern Medical Journal* 80, no. 7 (August): 886.

McCoy, Edain. 1995. *In A Graveyard at Midnight: Folk Magic and Wisdom from the Heart of Appalachia*. St. Paul, MN: Llewellyn Publications.

Prower, Tomás. 2015. *La Santa Muerte: Unearthing the Magic & Mysticism of Death*. Woodbury, MN: Llewellyn Publications.

Purcell Guild, June. 2011. *Black Laws of Virginia*. Westminster, MD: Heritage Books, Inc.

"Our Lady of Guadalupe or Tonantzin?" 2014. *The Yucatan Times,* December 11, 2014. http://www.theyucatantimes.com/2014/12/our-lady-of-guadalupe-or-tonantzin/.

Raboteau, Albert J. 2004. *Slave Religion: The Invisible Institution in the Antebellum South*. New York: Oxford University Press.

Randolph, Vance. 2003. *Ozark Magic and Folklore*. New York: Dover Publications.

Richmond, Nancy, and Misty Murray Walkup. 2011. *Appalachian Folklore: Omens, Signs and Superstitions*. North Charleston, SC: CreateSpace Independent Publishing Platform.

Rooks, Judith P. 2014. "The History of Midwifery." *Our Bodies Ourselves.* Updated May 22, 2014.

"Root Doctors." Gale Library of Daily Life: Slavery in America. Encyclopedia.com Accessed October 5, 2017.

Sennott, Br. Thomas Mary. 1997. "Infrared Study: An Analysis." In *A Handbook on Guadalupe* by Franciscan Friars of the Imaculate. New Bedford, MA: Academy of the Immaculate.

Smith, Theophus H. 1994. *Conjuring Culture: Biblical Formations of Black America*. New York: Oxford University Press.

Spence, Lewis. *2003. he Magic and Mysteries of Mexico: Or, the Arcane Secrets and Occult Lore of the Ancient Mexicans and Maya*. Whitefish, MT: Kessinger.

Suttlefilm. 2012. "Women of These Hills - 3 Cultures of Appalachia - 2000." YouTube.

Torres, Eliseo "Cheo", and Timothy L. Sawyer Jr. 2014. *Curandero: A Life in Mexican Folk Healing*. Albuquerque: University of New Mexico Press.

Trotter II, Robert T., and Juan Antonio Chavira. 1997. *Curanderismo: Mexican American Folk Healing*. Athens, GA: University of Georgia Press.

Washington, Harriet A. 2008. *Medical Apartheid: The Dark History of Medical Experimentation on Black Americans from Colonial Times to the Present*. New York: Anchor Books.

INDEX

To Write the Author

If you wish to contact the author or would like more information about this book, please write to the author in care of Llewellyn Worldwide, and we will forward your request. Both the author and publisher appreciate hearing from you and learning of your enjoyment of this book and how it has helped you. Llewellyn Worldwide cannot guarantee that every letter written to the author can be answered, but all will be forwarded. Please write to:

Katrina Rasbold
℅ Llewellyn Worldwide
2143 Wooddale Drive
Woodbury, MN 55125-2989

Please enclose a self-addressed stamped envelope for reply, or $1.00 to cover costs. If outside the USA, enclose an international postal reply coupon.